about the authors

Jan Purser and Kathy Snowball are the authors  von a
2006 Cordon d'Or Cookbooks and Culinar..., ... ine Illustrated
Cookbook category.

Jan is a naturopathic nutrition consultant, remedial therapist and meditation teacher.
Jan's passion is teaching people how to become more balanced holistically through nutrition, diet, detoxification programs, counselling, meditation and natural therapies. Her
busy clinic, Food, Body & Health is based in Perth. Jan has worked in the food and food
publishing industry for over 20 years and has been a practitioner since 1996. She is
currently the contributing health editor to *Australian Good Taste* magazine. Jan has written six books on health, food and meditation and her most recent books are *Indian
Home Cooking* (with Ajoy Joshi) and *Blender Drinks* (with Dimitra Stais and Tracey
Rutherford).

Kathy, a former food director of *Australian Gourmet Traveller*, is a freelance food
writer, menu and marketing consultant and educator. After a successful career in mer-
chant banking, Kathy went to London to study at Leith's School of Food and Wine. Eight
years of catering and teaching later, she returned home and joined the *Australian
Women's Weekly* as assistant food editor. She then became part of the *Gourmet
Traveller* team, becoming food editor in 1993 and food director in 2000. She has edited two cookbooks, *Gourmet Menus* and *Food for Friends*. Kathy is a partner in Manna
from Heaven, bakers of divine handmade biscuits and cakes.

the eat well cookbook

jan purser & kathy snowball

photography by greg elms

ALLEN & UNWIN

Front cover: Grilled Kofta with Pomegranate & Parsley Salad (page 52)
Back cover: Old-fashioned Trifle (page 139)

First published in 2006
Copyright text, © Jan Purser & Kathy Snowball 2006
Copyright photography, © Greg Elms 2006

Allen & Unwin Pty Ltd
83 Alexander Street
Crows Nest NSW 2065
Australia
Phone: (61 2) 8425 0100
Fax: (61 2) 9906 2218
Email: info@allenandunwin.com
Web: www.allenandunwin.com

National Library of Australia
Cataloguing-in-publication entry:
Purser, Jan.

    The eat well cookbook : gluten-free and dairy-free recipes for food lovers.
    1st ed.
    Includes index.

    ISBN 978 1 74114 827 5.
    ISBN 1 74114 827 8.

    1. Gluten-free diet - Recipes. 2. Milk-free diet - Recipes.
    I. Snowball, Kathy. II. Title.

Designed and typeset by Nada Backovic
Photography by Greg Elms
Food prepared by Celia Dowzer
Food styled by Virginia Dowzer
Edited by Kim Rowney
Index by Fay Donlevy
Printed in Singapore by Imago

contents

about the book

First and foremost, *The Eat Well Cookbook* is a collection of recipes, with sensational food suitable for all occasions whether it be dinner for two, a family meal or entertaining for the masses. The bonus is that it has been written with those of you in mind who like to keep a close eye on your health, weight and wellbeing but who also wish to eat really well. An even bigger bonus is that all the food is gluten- and dairy-free, for those of you with sensitivities or intolerances and allergies in those areas.

We are dear friends, sharing a great passion for food and the desire for good health. Both of us bring different expertise to the book: Kathy has a wealth of cooking knowledge and Jan brings her naturopathic knowledge. This food is real — it's what we cook and eat on a daily basis to keep us fit and full of vitality. Because it's real and because we live our philosophy, we know it works and that it can also work for you.

Many people ask us how we stay passionate about food and keep ourselves motivated to cook fabulous meals. For a start, we both exercise almost every day of the week and we are certain this increases our energy and optimism. With good energy and a positive outlook, we can't help but feel inspired to do the things that make us feel great. Added to that, we eat a wide range of foods and avoid those that don't suit our bodies. As a result, we enjoy good health and feel energetic most of the time.

We would dearly love you to adopt our philosophy, enjoy our way of cooking and eating wonderful food so that you can live a long, healthy and vital life.

our stories

JAN: Being a naturopathic nutrition consultant makes me very aware that more and more people are developing health problems because they eat too much of the same foods or choose the wrong types of foods. I also see the results of increased stress taking its toll. My clients are usually at a loss as to what to do about their symptoms, which range from digestive upsets to fatigue, headaches and skin rashes. I always start them on our detox program, outlined in our *Detox Cookbook*, to give their body a rest from potential problem foods. It's wonderful for me to see the changes in my clients' health and outlook as they progress through the detox. They feel more in control of their health because they finally get in touch with their bodies and can pinpoint what foods contribute to them feeling unwell, and what makes them feel good.

My own history includes a dairy sensitivity and I'm convinced that this exacerbated my childhood ear infections and subsequent hearing problems. I know that when I avoid dairy and keep wheat to a minimum my health and energy are excellent.

Understanding the foods that are right for your body is a great start to good health but feeling well is about so much more than just what you eat. I think that total good health means your physical body is well cared for, your emotional and mental selves are 'fed' and kept in balance, and your spiritual side is nurtured in whatever way makes you feel connected with others, the universe and nature. When all these facets are kept in balance, life is truly fabulous and life's challenges are generally more manageable.

KATHY: I think we all agree that if we feel fabulous, we have a better quality of life. As a food writer and part owner of the bakery, Manna from Heaven, I am very aware of the pitfalls of working in a food-related industry. While I want to enjoy the best food on offer, I also want to keep a watchful eye on my health, weight and general wellbeing. I would never pretend to be an expert on the path to good health, but after years of regular detoxing under Jan's guidance, I am very much in touch with my body and what suits it. I know that after a month of cutting out all wheat and dairy products while I'm detoxing, I feel light and energetic. I am not allergic to these foods, and I love wheat products, especially good bread, but I know that excessive indulgence in them will leave me feeling bloated and lethargic.

Good health and wellbeing is not just about what you eat. I walk with my dog Saffy every morning and swim three times a week. Don't get the wrong idea – I am not a fanatic. I exercise because I like it and it makes me feel good. Making time for relaxation is also important, and I'm an avid reader. But cooking is my favourite pastime of all. I never cook food just because it is good for me – I only ever cook food I love to eat. Our shared passion for good food is the basis for the recipes in this cookbook.

10 ways to eat well

Start with great ingredients that are fresh, flavour-filled and vital — no one wants to die of boredom trying to keep healthy. Next, look at how good the food is for you and what nutritional value it offers. Eating well means choosing the right mix of foods to provide the best nutrients to allow your body to maintain tip top health so you feel full of energy all day, every day.

1. **Eat seasonally**. Fruit and vegetables are at their nutritional best and have optimum flavour when they are in season, and provide the best nutrients for that time of year. For example, fruit and vegetables high in vitamin C are plentiful in autumn and winter, giving us a natural defence against colds and flu. If you buy organic fruit and vegetables, you will notice you can usually only buy varieties that are in season at the time. Aim to drink a fresh vegetable juice a couple of times a week, particularly those containing carrot and beetroot as these vegetables contain protective anti-oxidants that reduce the risk of disease.

2. **Avoid processed foods** wherever possible — fresh foods will provide the best nutrition for your body. Some processed foods, such as canned tomatoes, noodles, rice products and canned fish, are a great addition to the pantry but we suggest that you avoid processed snack foods and those that are high in kilojoules and low in beneficial nutrients. Processed foods are often high in salt, which can lead to fluid retention and is certainly not good for those of you with high blood pressure. Processed food may also contain preservatives, some of which are thought to be carcinogenic when consumed too often. If you have food intolerances or allergies, focusing on fresh foods, particularly organic and free-range, may help.

3. **Cook simple food with lots of flavour.** This could easily be our mantra because we love food that isn't too fussy but has loads of great flavour from fabulous fresh produce. A well-stocked pantry is important, so keep a good range of spices on hand, and always have a supply of garlic, ginger, chillies and onions at the ready. Consider growing your own herbs — oregano, chives, bay leaves, rosemary, sage, thyme, parsley and basil are all easy to grow and don't require much space.

4. **Avoid unhealthy takeaways.** When you simply do not have time to cook, choose a healthy takeaway meal. We buy dishes such as sushi combination and seaweed salad, teriyaki chicken or fish with rice and salad, Chinese steamed chicken with gai lan in oyster sauce or sambal and rice, Vietnamese fresh rice paper rolls and vegetable stir-fry, Vietnamese beef pho (beef and noodle soup), Chinese barbecued pork with stir-fry vegetables and rice, Indian dhal, rice and green beans, Indian beef vindaloo and rice (make a salad to go with it) or Chinese braised tofu and mushrooms with vegetables and rice. Note that there is no mention of pizza, burgers, fries or crumbed chicken on this list. This is for a good reason: these fast foods are very high in fat and salt and, when eaten regularly, will contribute to an increase in weight.

5. **Focus on your wellbeing, not your weight**. Avoid becoming obsessive about your weight and instead, put that energy into monitoring how you feel. When you choose foods specifically to help you feel better from an energy and emotion perspective, your weight will usually adjust to what is healthy for you. This might entail doing a detox twice a year, avoiding foods that make you feel sluggish (such as sugary and fatty foods), taking supplements that boost your energy and eating well balanced meals to keep your energy levels stable (helping you avoid sugar cravings and energy slumps). See page 10 for 10 Ways to Reduce and Manage your Weight.

6. **Have three well-balanced meals a day**. This means eating a balance of protein, carbohydrate and fat. The right combination will give you sustained energy during the day, will make you feel less like snacking and will provide a good range of essential nutrients. See the Eat Well Food Plan on page 4.

7. **Go for low GI carbs.** When you eat carbohydrates, make them low glycaemic index (GI) where possible. Low GI carbohydrates are broken down and absorbed by your digestive system more slowly, providing sustained energy for a longer time. This helps reduce sugar cravings and helps you feel energetic all day. When combined with protein, it reduces the likelihood of snacking unnecessarily. Some examples of gluten-free low GI carbohydrate foods are: sweet potatoes, basmati rice, gluten-free hi-fibre bread, fresh rice noodles, legumes (lentils, chickpeas, beans), soy milk, soy yoghurt, buckwheat, gluten-free muesli, corn on the cob, fresh corn kernels lightly cooked, nuts and seeds. Higher GI carbohydrates, such as rice other than basmati, white gluten-free bread, rice cakes, polenta, white potatoes, puffed rice or millet and dried rice noodles can be eaten, but be sure to team them with some protein and fibre (in the form of vegetables, fruit or salad) which help to make the overall GI of a meal lower. For more information on low GI foods, look at *The New Glucose Revolution*, Professor Jenny Brand-Miller, Kaye Foster-Powell and Professor Stephen Colagiuri (Hodder, 2002)

8. **Put less food on your plate**. Large dinner plates can look great but might tempt you to serve up larger portions, so think about using smaller plates. There seems to be an obvious correlation between our population becoming larger and the tendency towards larger serving sizes and snack bar sizes. Help yourself maintain a good weight by thinking 'small' when it comes to portions but thinking 'big' when it comes to vegetables and salad.

9. **Create a good environment to eat in**. Part of the enjoyment of eating well is making a point of creating time to enjoy your food and to unwind from the day. We love sitting at a set table and relaxing over the evening meal, catching up with the events in our partner's lives. Don't have the television on – it is neither good for communication nor digestion – but choose some relaxing music. Ignore the telephone and treat the evening meal as an occasion, every day.

10. **Don't eat when you are distressed**. This will most likely lead to digestive problems, so try to put off eating until you feel calmer. See page 17 for some techniques to help you manage stress, diffuse overwhelming emotions and create a calmer state of mind. If you are going through an emotionally stressful time, seek the help of your naturopath who may prescribe some very effective herbal or nutritional supplements to reduce the effects of stress on your body.

the eat well food plan

This is a guide on what to eat at each meal so you are eating a good mix of nutrients, ensuring that you feel energetic and reducing the likelihood of sugar cravings and mid-afternoon energy slumps. This will help you to sustain good energy. An easy way to judge the appropriate protein and carbohydrate portions for your body is to look at your palm size and thickness (referred to as your palm's volume). Go to our seasonal menu plans on pages 172-3 for ideas on how to plan your week's meals using the recipes in this book.

BREAKFAST

Include the following food types:

Freshly made vegetable juice or a large glass of warm water with the juice of half a lemon squeezed into it.

Protein – choose from eggs, nuts and seeds, fish, chicken, tofu, meat, soy cheese, legumes (chickpeas, beans, lentils), protein powder (see glossary), soy yoghurt (this supplies a little protein along with carbohydrate). Include a small portion of protein with your breakfast (60-80 gm or about half your palm's volume).

Carbohydrate – yeast-free hi-fibre bread, corn bread, cooked rice, rice or corn crispbread, soy or rice milk, puffed cereal (rice, corn, millet), rolled oats (if you tolerate them), rolled rice, nut and seed muesli, cooked potato, soy yoghurt, buckwheat pancakes. Have $\frac{1}{2}$ to 1 cup carbohydrate (or 1 to $1\frac{1}{2}$ times your palm's volume).

Fat – this will already be present in nuts, seeds, cereals, eggs, soy yoghurt, hi-fibre bread, corn bread and muesli. You need just a little.

Fibre – breakfast is a good time to include a high-fibre food such as ground linseeds or psyllium husks to help with regularity.

Fruit and/or vegetable – if you like, save your fruit for between meals, or have some with breakfast. Some of our breakfast recipes include a vegetable.

LUNCH

Include the following food types:

Protein – in addition to the breakfast protein list, try venison, duck, quail, lamb or shellfish. Have a portion of a protein food to suit your appetite (or $1/2$ to 1 times your palm's volume).

Carbohydrate – in addition to the breakfast list, look for starchy vegetables (potato, sweet potato, corn), rice noodles, buckwheat noodles, cooked buckwheat, quinoa, amaranth and polenta. Have 1 to 2 slices of hi-fibre yeast-free bread, 2 to 4 rice or corn crispbread, or the equivalent of $1/2$ to 1 cup cooked carbohydrate (or 1 to $1^1/2$ times your palm's volume).

Fat – as for breakfast, there may already be a little fat in the protein food choice. But you can also have a little drizzle of extra virgin oil or a nut or avocado oil over salad or vegetables (this may be in the form of a dressing).

Vegetables, raw and/or cooked – have the equivalent of 2 to 3 cups of non-starchy vegetables, preferably different colours.

Fruit

DINNER

Protein – as for breakfast and lunch.

Have a portion of a protein food to suit your appetite (1 times your palm's volume).

Carbohydrate – as for breakfast and lunch.

Have the equivalent of $1/2$ to $3/4$ cup ($1/2$-1 times your palm's volume).

Fat – as for breakfast and lunch.

Vegetables – as for lunch. Have 3 to 4 cups of different coloured non-starchy vegetables.

Fruit – you may like to finish your meal with a piece of fruit, or have a light dessert occasionally.

SNACKS

Choose from the following: a piece or two of fresh fruit, a small handful of nuts and seeds, one or two corn or rice crispbread spread with hummus or some sort of nut spread, a small container of soy yoghurt (you can mix this with fruit and/or nuts and seeds), a cup of raw vegetable sticks plain or with a little hummus.

10 ways to manage food sensitivities and allergies

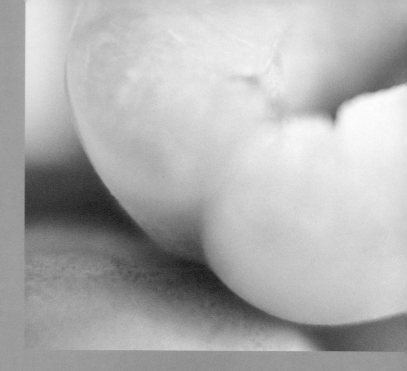

A food allergy is an immune response to a specific food, usually to the protein component. A food sensitivity or intolerance (much more common than a true allergy) is a chemical reaction to a food, usually to the various components in foods and additives.

Some food allergy reactions are severe, resulting in drastic symptoms such as sudden hives or an asthma attack, and can even be life-threatening where the heart and lungs shut down. In these cases, the offending food is avoided at all costs. However, many food allergy symptoms and food sensitivity or intolerance symptoms are very similar.

People can develop food allergy or sensitivities to all kinds of foods and it is not uncommon to develop them in your thirties and beyond, despite not reacting to a food before then. Chronic stress, poor diet or poor digestion can gradually diminish your immune function, making your body more prone to potential food and environmental allergens.

In coeliac disease, the allergy is to the protein, or gluten, in wheat, rye, spelt, barley and triticale. Oats may also be a problem for some people due to contamination from the other grains mentioned. The symptoms range from severe gastrointestinal distress to fatigue, anaemia and a feeling of poor health. Gluten must be totally avoided regardless of whether the symptoms subside after eliminating it, because over time, the allergic reaction leads to damage of the small intestine wall, impairing digestion and nutrient absorption, resulting in nutrient deficiencies and malnutrition.

Dairy allergy (usually to the protein casein), or dairy sensitivity or intolerance (usually to the milk sugar lactose) can result in any of the symptoms listed opposite.

It is possible that you may tolerate a suspect food on its own, but not in combination with other suspect foods – the allergen load may tip you over the symptom-free threshold.

testing for allergy, sensitivities or intolerance

Most testing procedures – blood tests, skin prick tests and muscle testing – are not conclusive, although they certainly give a good indication of foods to watch. A wheat allergy can be determined by a blood test, and coeliac disease by small intestine biopsy.

The most conclusive way of determining whether you react to a food is to eliminate the suspect food or foods for at least two weeks or until symptoms abate. Then 'challenge' your body by re-introducing the foods one at a time, noting any physical symptoms or side effects, or changes in energy levels and mood. It can help to avoid any foods that you react to strongly for several months, then very gradually re-introduce them into your diet and have them only occasionally. This is often the most effective way of reducing reactions. At the same time, it is crucial that you build your digestion strength and immune function to ensure your body is less reactive overall and becomes symptom-free.

Symptoms for allergies, sensitivities and intolerances may include any of the following:

runny nose	irritable bowel syndrome	chronic cystitis
skin rash	ulcerative colitis	fluid retention
diarrhoea	bed wetting in children	acne
vomiting	sweating	bloating
nausea	palpitations	fatigue
itching	feeling shaky	chronic colds
burning or swelling around	nervousness	recurring ear infections
the mouth	headache	anxiety
abdominal cramps	migraine	depression
mouth ulcers	rapid breathing	poor sleep
flatulence	burning sensations on the skin	inability to concentrate
gastritis	eczema	

If you suspect you have a food allergy or sensitivity, try keeping a food diary (see page 8) to see if there is a link between the foods you are eating and how you are feeling. If you experience any of these on an on-going basis, seek advice from a health professional.

1. **Seek professional advice.** If you suspect you have a food allergy or intolerance, it is best to enlist the help of a qualified nutrition consultant, naturopath or dietician to help you with an elimination diet which omits suspect foods, followed by a challenge program of re-introducing the foods to gauge your response. Some elimination diets are very restrictive, so it is important to do this correctly for best results. Your practitioner may prescribe nutritional or herbal support to strengthen your digestion and immune function based on your symptoms and medical history.

2. **Improve your digestion.** Naturopaths believe that, aside from chronic stress and poor diet, bowel permeability (also called 'leaky gut syndrome'), bowel toxicity, low production of stomach acid and insufficiency of pancreatic enzymes can play a role in the development of food allergy or intolerance. Non-steroidal anti-inflammatory medication and cortisone-based medication are also thought to have an effect while a long history of antibiotic use can compromise the digestive system. Firstly, make sure you chew your food thoroughly, taking your time to eat. This will help to improve your digestion, allowing your brain to receive and send signals so that the appropriate enzymes and acids are produced in adequate quantities to break down and absorb the food you are eating. Secondly, it can be helpful to take digestive bitters in water or a digestive bitters tablet before meals, or a digestive enzyme tablet with meals to improve your digestion. Your naturopath will be able to help you decide which you need. This ensures that you are treating both the cause and the symptoms to get the best long-term results.

3. **Avoid getting into a food rut.** To avoid developing any, or further, food intolerances, make sure you eat a wide variety of all the food types. It is best not to buy and eat the same foods week in and week out. Vary the food you eat at all your meals and don't have the same food more than once a day if possible. If you have a food intoler-ance, it can be useful to make a point of eating that food only every three or four days. If you eat foods like dairy products, wheat, eggs, oranges, soy products or tomatoes every day, change your patterns to give them a rest on a regular basis as these are some of the most common food allergens.

4. **Do a detox once or twice a year.** Our detox program, detailed in our *Detox Cookbook*, is essentially a well-balanced modified elimination regime that gives your body a break from many potential food allergens. Make sure you also omit any additional foods you suspect affect you. A detox program with appropriate nutritional and herbal supplements can help to strengthen your immune function and digestion, minimising your reactions to foods.

5. **Have a variety of grain foods.** Because gluten is found in many common grain foods and their products (wheat, rye, spelt, barley, triticale and oats), it makes good sense to bring in a variety of other grains and starchy carbohydrate foods to create variety. Many people eat wheat products several times a day (wheat based cereal, muffins, sandwiches, biscuits and pasta are common in the average diet) and it can be this monotony that results in an intolerance. Think outside the square. Other grain foods include corn, rice, quinoa, amaranth, arrowroot, sago, tapioca, buckwheat, millet, sorghum, and legume-based flours like chickpea, lentil and mung bean. Noodle varieties, aside from wheat-based pasta, include rice noodles, buckwheat noodles, mung bean noodles, spelt pasta (if you are okay with gluten) and gluten-free pasta. You can buy these foods from the health food and Asian sections of the supermarket and from health food stores.

6. **Take note of symptoms.** Keep a detailed food diary, noting everything you eat and drink along with how you feel each day, so that you can refer to the diary if you have any reactions. It is so easy to forget what you have eaten

the previous day, and reactions may not occur until the day following consumption of a problem food. Start your diary before you omit suspect foods and keep it up until after you have re-introduced them – it will be a great help in the long run. Once you have a few weeks of diaries, look for recurring patterns or reactions from the same types of foods, or products made from the same ingredients. Often you don't realise how often you may have a reaction until you keep a diary.

7. **Pay attention to cravings.** If you crave certain foods, particularly not-so-healthy foods such as chocolate, sweets or cakes, it may suggest that you are sensitive to those foods. The most common problem cravings are chocolate, alcohol, caffeine drinks, wheat-based foods like bread, cakes or biscuits, cheese and soft drinks. If you begin to crave these foods, take note of any symptoms after eating them – you may discover you have an intolerance to the very thing you think your body needs. Do keep in mind, though, that sometimes you might crave a food for its specific nutrients, such as craving meat because your iron is a little low – this can be a good thing.

8. **Eat a wide variety of foods** when pregnant. Many women believe that the food they eat during pregnancy will influence the risk of their baby developing food allergies later on. There is ample scientific evidence showing that this is not so, and it is best for a pregnant woman to eat a wide variety of foods to gain the best possible nutrition for her growing baby.

9. **Encourage children to eat a wide variety of foods.** If you have children, make sure they don't fall into a food rut. By bringing variety into their meals and mixing and matching the grain foods they eat, you can give them a great start. Children may be more susceptible to developing food intolerance for a number of reasons: poor digestion, a mineral or vitamin deficiency or a mineral imbalance (excess copper in relation to zinc is thought to make them more prone to allergic reactions). If you suspect any of these, seek the help of your naturopath to improve their health while they are young. If your child has developed eczema you may want to keep a food diary of their diet for a few weeks, noting symptoms of food intolerance and cravings that could indicate potential problem foods. Encourage your children to sit while eating, and to chew well without rushing. It certainly helps to avoid having the television on during meals so they concentrate on eating properly.

10. **Take supplements to improve your health.** Your naturopath may prescribe the following to help build your gastrointestinal tract (GIT):

- vitamin C with bioflavonoids (to help reduce allergic reactions and acts as an anti-inflammatory agent),
- digestive bitters or enzymes (to improve GIT function),
- vitamin B complex (the Bs help with the breakdown and absorption of food),
- fructo-oligosaccharides (or FOS, provides the best kind of fibre that beneficial bacteria in the GIT thrive on, helping them to multiply, building the health of the GIT),
- colostrum (produced from whey or sourced from cattle, helps to build the immune system),
- arabinogalactans (helps build GIT strength),
- probiotics (beneficial bacteria, helps improve digestion, assists GIT repair and helps build immunity),
- fish oil (EFA and DHA) and evening primrose oil (reduces inflammation and helps GIT repair and strengthen),
- echinacea and astragalus (to boost immune function and lessen reactivity to allergens),
- homeopathic phenolic desensitisation drops (drops taken several times a day to reduce your reactions to allergens), and,
- selenium and zinc (minerals essential for healthy digestion and immune function).

10 ways to reduce and manage your weight

We want you to focus on how you feel, on what makes you feel good and to learn what doesn't suit your body. We don't recommend crash diets – going on and off diets will lead to the yo-yo syndrome where your body's metabolism drops every time, making maintaining a healthy weight all the more impossible. The only way to reach and maintain a healthy weight is by reviewing your eating and lifestyle habits and changing the ones that are not serving you well. We think of it as choosing to adopt lifestyle habits that will make you feel great.

1. **If you don't use it, you wear it.** This fact is based on simple maths. If you eat more kilojoules than your body can use, you'll store those kilojoules as fat. Doing this repeatedly leads to weight gain. We are not suggesting you start counting kilojoules, but recommend that you look at where you can consume less. You can increase your kilojoule usage by doing daily exercise and being more active.

   If you eat low kilojoules and still put on weight or cannot shift weight, seek the help of a health practitioner. You may have an underactive thyroid, insulin resistance or your body may be reacting to chronic stress. All of these can lead to weight gain.

2. **Have a regular Cellular Health Analysis (CHA) check.** CHA shows your muscle mass, body fat composition, biological age, cellular health and vitality, and toxicity and fluid retention in your body. Your CHA practitioner will be able to tell you what kind of exercise you specifically need to reduce your weight and improve your health. A CHA check will show if nutrients are being fully utilised by your body's cells. If they are not, your practitioner will help you remedy this and will also be able to tell you if you need particular nutrients to reduce fluid retention, inflammation or toxicity.

   If you have great health, a CHA check will help to keep you on track ensuring you age youthfully and continue to have an energetic life. A CHA check helps you to remain motivated as you make necessary changes to diet and lifestyle. There is no greater encouragement then seeing your biological age become younger, looking younger, seeing your body composition change for the better and feeling far more energetic.

3. **Avoid unnecessary kilojoules.** Avoid overdoing alcohol, fruit juice and eating high-kilojoule snacks. All of these add extra, unnecessary kilojoules into your daily intake. Read the nutrition information panel on foods you buy to determine the fat, sugars and kilojoules. It can be quite an eye opener. Remember the 95 per cent rule – it's what you do 95 per cent of the time that really counts. You can indulge in treats five per cent of the time and still maintain a healthy weight but indulge any more than that, and you had best get on your bike, or into those joggers.

4. **Assess your social eating habits.** If you have a busy social life you may tend to overeat when drinking alcohol and eating with friends. Balance your meals over the day to compensate for social eating. If you are dining out or entertaining at home then consider your other meals that day to balance your intake. For example, if dining out in the evening, eat a light breakfast such as a small bowl of nut and seed muesli, only have fruit for snacks and have a big salad with a protein food for lunch. This way you can indulge a little at dinner time without overdoing your kilojoule intake for the day. Perhaps skip dessert or share one to keep things in moderation.

5. **Recognise emotional eating.** This is where a lot of people lose the plot. When the stress levels crank up, you can fall into the trap of comfort eating – usually on high kilojoule or highly processed foods.

   Before reaching for that comfort food snack, ask yourself the following questions:

- Am I really hungry or is this a comfort eating urge?
- Why am I choosing it?
- Is there an emotional trigger?
- Am I eating due to boredom, habit, stress, loneliness?
- Is this related to an activity, such as watching television?
- What healthier food could I eat instead?
- Do I really need it?
- Am I truly prepared to add unnecessary kilojoules to my day and possibly store unnecessary fat?

Copy this and pop it on the refrigerator as a pre-snack check list. The only way to change comfort eating habits is to become aware of them and then replace them with another, more beneficial, action. If the urge to comfort eat is related to an activity such as watching television, do something else instead, such as read, do some stretch exercises, pursue your hobby, have a relaxing bath, listen to music or call a friend. Keep a record of your comfort eating urges so you can recognise the patterns you have developed. A good strategy when you have the comfort food urge is to eat something healthy, like a piece of fresh fruit, then, after 15 minutes, review whether you really need the comfort food. If you still do, then distract yourself by doing something active instead of giving in. Another good strategy is to only eat at the table. Never eat standing at the refrigerator or cupboard. Best of all, keep an honest food diary where you record everything you eat and drink and be accountable for it. You could include your comfort eating urges in your food diary so that you get to know what triggers those urges.

6. **Only eat when you are hungry** but don't skip meals. Many people tend to eat even if they are not hungry, mostly due to habit. If you don't tend to be hungry at meal times, review your snacking habits. Save your eating for actual meals. If you are often not hungry, you may need to increase your exercise or you may be choosing the wrong mix of foods. See our Eat Well Food Plan on page 4 for a guide to what to eat each day. If you skip meals on a regular basis, you run the risk of lowering your metabolic rate which means your body will burn fewer kilojoules and store the leftover as fat. At the very least, eat a good salad with a little protein at meal times to give your body the nutrients it needs and to keep your metabolism chugging along.

7. **Enjoy your meals** but don't eat the leftovers afterwards. Make delicious meals that are pleasurable to prepare and eat and take the time to sit down at the dining table to enjoy them. Never eat on the run or pick at food mindlessly. Pop any leftovers into a container in the refrigerator for lunch the next day.

8. **Stop eating when you begin to feel satisfied** and don't continue to eat until you feel overfull. This is an important point as we have so much food available in our society that it can be tempting to overindulge. It takes at least 20 minutes for our brain to get the message that we have eaten enough food. This is why it is important to take your time eating, so you can 'get the message' in time, before you have overeaten. Remember to think about portion sizes and leaving a little on your plate. Never go for second helpings and don't have dessert if you already feel full after the main course. If you can't possibly resist, then remember to eat lightly the next day to balance out the week.

9. **Use statements to achieve your goals.** Rid your mind of negative thoughts. You are not only what you eat, you are what you think about yourself. The thoughts you have about yourself and your body will influence your eating habits and lifestyle choices. If you constantly berate yourself or put yourself down, you are more likely to make poor food choices, exercise little and struggle to maintain a healthy weight.

Say this statement to yourself: 'I am overweight and I look horrible'. How do you feel inside when you say that? Do you notice that your energy seeps away just holding that thought? Now say this to yourself: 'I love eating well and feeling great!' How do you feel inside when you say that? Do you notice that your energy increases as you hold that thought?

Some further statements that will help you feel great are:

- 'I feel very good about myself and enjoy looking after my body'
- 'Every day I am getting better and better'
- 'I am fit, healthy and full of energy'

Place these statements where you can see them daily. Repeat them to yourself several times a day, even if at first you don't agree with the words. When you catch yourself having negative self thoughts, immediately say in your mind 'No!' or 'Stop!' and repeat a positive statement a few times. Continue to work on changing your thought patterns for the better and you will achieve your goals.

10. **Weigh yourself once a month** only or lose the scales forever if you feel addicted to weighing yourself. Many people jump on the scales each day and if the result is not favourable, they feel bad about themselves which starts off the comfort eating cycle. Scales are only a useful tool when they are used at regular intervals and at the same time each month (this is particularly the case for women whose hormone levels may influence fluid levels in their body). If you like, jot your weighing day in your diary and treat it as a challenge to yourself to be pleased with the reading each month. You really don't need to rely on scales because you can tell if a little weight has crept on, or if you have reduced any extra padding, by the feel of clothes and by looking in that full length mirror. Adopt our philosophy – become tuned in to your body so you will know when it does not feel as good as it could, then take measures to correct it accordingly.

10 ways to live well and feel great

Living well comes from achieving balance in all areas of your life. By balance we mean maintaining a good mental and emotional state as well as physical. Sometimes the balance can get way out of kilter due to all kinds of work, home or relationship pressures, but the secret is to notice the imbalance as quickly as you can then do what is needed to tip the scales back to an even footing before your health is affected. You will know when you are off balance when you: over react, feel overwhelmed, don't care about eating well, can't be bothered exercising, feel depressed, don't look forward to the day, don't experience little moments of joy, lose your sense of humour, lose a sense of purpose, start eating sugary foods, drink excess alcohol often, overdo caffeine, feel drained, cry at the drop of a hat, feel angry all the time, and, yell at the kids a lot. If any of this sounds like you, read our strategies for managing stress on page 17.

1. **Manage stress** – it is a major contributor to disease and ageing. When you are dealing with stress, your body produces stress hormones called adrenalin and cortisol. When stress is chronic, the oversupply of cortisol can make your body store fat more easily, particularly around your middle, markedly increasing the risk of developing diabetes and heart disease. It can certainly lead to a condition called insulin resistance, which, if left untreated, can result in diabetes. This condition can leave you feeling fatigued most of the time because your body cells do not receive enough glucose needed for energy. If you have a chubby middle, then see your naturopath or practitioner to check if you have insulin resistance and take steps to correct the condition.

2. **Maintain a healthy weight.** Excess weight, aside from increasing the risk of diabetes and heart diseases, creates stress on your body that can hasten degenerative changes in major joints such as the knees and hips, leading to arthritis. When you maintain a healthy weight, you will have more energy, will remain youthful for longer and your body will be much healthier in every way. Look at our weight-reducing strategies on page 10.

3. **Exercise most days of the week.** Not only is exercise an excellent way to manage stress, it also helps to: reduce and prevent depression; lower your risk of developing diabetes, heart disease and cancer; and slows the ageing process. It may interest you to know that muscle loss and fat storage due to inactivity is a major biomarker of ageing. Reversing both can increase your longevity very nicely. When your body is fit and your muscles are toned, you have much greater energy to thrive on and can enjoy life to the max.

4. **Get good quality sleep.** If anxiety is preventing or disturbing your sleep, follow our stress management strategies on page 17. Sleep is the number one 'battery recharger'. Poor sleep, or lack of sleep, means your energy reserves cannot be well replenished and can lead to exhaustion, excess stress and depression. You need around seven to eight hours sleep each night to ensure you feel vital and vibrant.

5. **Reward yourself often.** We both work very hard yet still make a point of doing things we find uplifting. We find it crucial to our sense of wellbeing. Everyone enjoys different rewards but think about visiting art galleries, seeing a good movie, dining out, going to the theatre, having weekends away, going to the beach, going shopping, taking time out to read, cooking great meals, going for a stroll, and having a decent holiday break every year. Rewards take us away from the demands of daily life and help us recharge our batteries ready for the next busy time ahead.

6. **Spend time with other people.** Many people tend to cut themselves off socially if they are overly busy. We are not meant to be 'islands' and isolation can lead to depression. Make sure you factor time into your life for your family and friends as this will help keep you emotionally balanced. Remember the importance of having a good laugh – it is very therapeutic, and the best opportunities for laughter come from spending time with other people.

7. **Keep a positive attitude.** If you keep up with exercise, give yourself regular rewards and eat well, a positive attitude is pretty easy to achieve. It is well known that you get more of what you focus on. If you focus on how fortunate you are to have good

health and a good life, you get more of the same. Likewise, if you focus on what's lacking in your life you will attract more dissatisfaction. If you feel yourself spiralling into the abyss of negative thinking, do what you can to pull yourself out. Look at our managing stress strategies on page 17 or read about using positive statements on page 13. Having a good laugh will pull you out of the blues, as will some strenuous exercise. It also helps to look at the big picture. We can so easily become bogged down by the petty things in life and forget to appreciate the little joyous moments. Make sure you spend time with people who are positive as those negative ones will always drag your energy down, leaving you feel drained. Negativity is quite catching, but so is optimism.

8. **Strive to be successful and enjoy what you do.** Follow your passion and you will find your pursuits truly rewarding. This is such an important element of feeling great, as you would know if you have ever worked in a job that you don't enjoy. It can be quite debilitating to your body, mind and spirit to remain stuck in a situation such as this. If you feel it's impossible to change your job situation, then follow your passion through your hobbies and in your spare time. Who knows, it may eventually lead to great changes in your life. Being successful doesn't mean anything more than feeling pleased with what you have accomplished as you review your day before you go to sleep at night. Whatever you are doing, strive to do it to the best of your abilities as this is an essential part of building self-esteem and feelings of self-worth. You will feel great if you have healthy self-esteem and value what you have to offer.

9. **Have several alcohol free days (AFDs) each week.** It is good practice to give your body a break from alcohol every week. Many people feel more energetic if they abstain during the working week. Alcohol is a depressant and should be avoided if you are feeling flat or depressed. Alcohol also adds quite a few kilojoules into your day and can cause your weight to slowly creep up if those kilojoules are not used for energy. There are lots of pluses as a result of cutting down alcohol, but there are also lots of pluses from enjoying a very good drop of wine. As with everything, balance is the key.

10. **Take some basic supplements.** Your body will function more efficiently if you have a good multivitamin and mineral supplement every day. If you are prone to sore joints or arthritis, add in a supplement containing glucosamine, which is excellent joint food. If you have inflammation, then fish oil (EPA/DHA) is essential for its anti-inflammatory properties. Finally, some daily fibre in the form of psyllium husks will help to keep you regular and will help lower your blood cholesterol. Your naturopath will also be able to advise you on specific supplements for any particular health condition you may have.

strategies for managing general stress

Eat well. Don't give in to cravings for sugary, fatty processed foods as they will make you feel worse.

Exercise daily. Both aerobic and weight resistance exercise are effective in reducing insulin resistance and they stimulate the release of endorphins, or feel-good hormones, in the brain.

Avoid alcohol.

Take time out each day to relax, doing something you enjoy.

Have a good laugh. Laughing, like exercise, releases endorphins.

Breathe deeply. When you are stressed you tend to take shallow breaths and this creates a physical stress. Remind yourself to take long slow deep breaths that fill your lungs and expand your abdomen. Practise inhaling and exhaling for a longer time to gain the full benefits of the relaxation and stress release.

Listen to soothing music.

Have a regular massage. Part of your body's stress response is that you will hold tension in your muscles. Most people find their back, shoulder and neck muscles are most affected.

Stretch tense muscles each day, particularly if your work involves sitting down most of the day writing or at your computer.

JAN: *I always go for a walk on the beach (and a swim in summer) before breakfast which makes a wonderful start to the day. I tend to have a protein powder and berry smoothie (based on soy or rice milk, rice protein or isolated whey protein and berries) with a small bowl of gluten-free muesli in summer or porridge in winter. That mix keeps me chugging along nicely all through the morning. I might have a few nuts or a piece of fruit mid-morning, but I am usually too busy at the clinic. I focus on eating this good balance of nutrients to keep my energy levels stable during the day so that I don't fall in a heap at the end. It makes an amazing difference to eat this way (see Ten Ways To Eat Well, page x) and my clients always comment on how good they feel when they change their habits.*

KATHY: *When I first met Jan (about 15 years ago), I used to skip breakfast or just grab an apple on the run, and wondered why I always felt so run down. It's still not my favourite meal of the day, but after listening to Jan, I now think about it more and make sure I eat something substantial in the morning, and it's not surprising that I feel so much better for it. In winter I love porridge with banana or rhubarb and in summer, our gluten-free Nut & Seed Muesli (page 22) with seasonal fruit, such as mango or peaches, and soy milk. Like Jan, I rise early and walk and swim in the mornings, plus drink lots of water. Water is a key element of my diet and I drink at least 2 litres (64 fl oz) a day. It keeps me hydrated and works wonders for my ageing skin.*

breakfast

One major mistake people make is to skip breakfast. This meal is terribly important because it helps to rev up your metabolism after the 'fast' during the night. If you can't face breakfast early, then make your breakfast time a bit later or at least start the day with an easy-to-drink protein powder and fruit smoothie. If you miss breakfast, or any other meal, your metabolism is likely to slow down a little which makes putting on weight much more likely.

We have covered most bases in this section, from more substantial weekend breakfast dishes, to lighter weekday options.

If you eat breakfast out, try to avoid greasy bacon and sausages, as these will only add to your waistline, not to mention your cholesterol levels. If you must indulge, then do so but only on the odd occasion.

Another important morning tip is to drink a couple of large glasses of water to hydrate your body. This can be in the form of herbal tea or water with a squeeze of lemon or lime juice if you like.

buckwheat & blueberry soufflé pancakes with scented hazelnut syrup

People who love pancakes can enjoy this recipe without being overly concerned about their waistline. This makes a special breakfast or brunch for lazy weekends or holidays.

1 cup (5 oz) gluten-free
   self-raising flour

1 cup (5 oz) buckwheat flour

2 tbsp gluten-free gluten substitute

2 tsp gluten-free baking powder

1/2 tsp ground cinnamon

20 g (3/4 oz) hazelnut meal

1 1/4 cups (10 fl oz) low-fat soy
   or rice milk

4 eggs, separated

1 tbsp pure maple syrup

1 1/2 cups (7 oz) fresh or
   thawed frozen blueberries

macadamia oil, to grease

SCENTED HAZELNUT SYRUP

1/3 cup (1 3/4 oz) hazelnuts

2 cups (16 fl oz) unsweetened
   100% apple juice

1 vanilla bean, split lenghtwise

3 cm (1 1/4 in) piece
   cinnamon stick

1 1/2 tbsp pure maple syrup

To make Scented Hazelnut Syrup, spread hazelnuts on an oven tray and toast at 180°C (350°F) for 7–8 minutes or until lightly browned and fragrant. Place nuts in a clean tea towel and rub vigorously to remove skins. Roughly chop the nuts and set aside.

Bring apple juice, vanilla and cinnamon to the boil in a saucepan over medium heat. Simmer, uncovered, for 8–10 minutes or until reduced by half. Stir in hazelnuts and maple syrup and set aside to cool slightly.

Sift flour, buckwheat flour, gluten substitute, baking powder and cinnamon into a large bowl. Stir in hazelnut meal and make a well in the centre.

Whisk together milk, 1/3 cup (2 1/2 fl oz) water, egg yolks and maple syrup. Gradually stir into the flour mixture and whisk to a smooth batter. Stir in blueberries.

Use electric beaters to whisk egg whites in a clean bowl until firm peaks form. Gently fold egg whites into pancake batter until combined.

Heat a large non-stick frying pan over medium heat and brush with oil. Use a 1/3 cup measure to scoop two lots of pancake batter into pan, allowing room for spreading. Cook for 2 minutes or until browned underneath. Carefully turn pancakes and cook for 2 minutes or until puffed, browned underneath and cooked through. Line an oven tray with baking paper and place pancakes on tray in oven at 100°C (200°F) to keep warm. Repeat with remaining batter to make 12 pancakes, lightly brushing pan with oil between batches.

To serve, place pancakes on serving plates and drizzle the syrup over the top.

SERVES 4–6

Batter can be made several hours ahead – whisk egg whites and fold through just before cooking. Pancakes will keep warm in oven for up to an hour. Syrup will keep for up to 1 week in refrigerator.

GLUTEN-FREE ✔ DAIRY-FREE ✔ DETOX-FRIENDLY ✔

creamy bircher muesli

Bircher muesli in its original form was little more than oats and grated apple. Thankfully, it has evolved into something with infinite variations. This one is gluten-free, made with cooked rice instead of oats. If you like, add a teaspoon or two of protein powder to the muesli or serve with a small protein powder drink for a more substantial start to the day.

1 large Granny Smith apple, unpeeled,
   halved, cored, coarsely grated

1²/₃ cups (8 oz) cooked medium-grain rice

200 g (6¹/₂ oz) carton vanilla soy yoghurt

¹/₃ cup (2¹/₂ fl oz) soy or rice milk

2 tbsp sultanas

2 tbsp lemon juice

2 tsp psyllium husks

¹/₄ cup (1¹/₂ oz) slivered almonds, toasted

2 tbsp pepitas (pumpkin seeds)

¹/₃ cup (1¹/₂ oz) fresh blueberries or other
   fresh fruit, to serve

Combine apple, rice, yoghurt, milk, sultanas, lemon juice and psyllium in a bowl. Mix well. Cover and place in the refrigerator overnight to soak.

Before serving, stir almonds and pepitas into the rice mixture and spoon into bowls. Top with fruit and serve.

SERVES 2

Muesli mixture will keep in an airtight container in refrigerator for up to 2 days. Add the nuts and seeds just before serving.

GLUTEN-FREE ✔ DAIRY-FREE ✔ DETOX-FRIENDLY ✔

nut & seed muesli

This muesli is rich in fibre and nutrients, so just a small serve will keep you satisfied and full of energy throughout the morning. We used a selection of preservative-free dried fruit – apple, strawberries, wild figs and pineapple – but you can use any preservative-free dried fruit of your choice. Serve with soy or rice milk and a dollop of soy yoghurt if you like, topped with some fresh fruit such as berries, mango or banana. If you can eat oats (they are not gluten-free), you could use 1 cup of oats in place of puffed rice.

2 1/2 cups (6 oz) rice bran flakes

1 cup (1 3/4 oz) puffed rice

1 cup (6 1/2 oz) whole buckwheat

1 cup (1 1/2 oz) flaked coconut

1 cup (3 1/2 oz) flaked almonds

1 cup firmly packed (3 1/2 oz) chopped
  preservative-free dried fruit

1/2 cup (2 1/2 oz) sultanas

1/2 cup (2 1/2 oz) brazil nuts, sliced

1/2 cup (2 1/2 oz) pepitas (pumpkin seeds)

1/2 cup (2 1/4 oz) sunflower seeds

1/2 cup (2 1/4 oz) linseeds (flax seeds)

1/2 cup (2 1/2 oz) lecithin

Combine all ingredients in a large airtight container.

MAKES ABOUT 9 1/2 CUPS

Muesli will keep in an airtight container in a cool cupboard
for up to 2 months.

GLUTEN-FREE ✔   DAIRY-FREE ✔   DETOX-FRIENDLY ✔

potato cakes with wilted spinach & poached eggs

To speed things along a bit, you can steam the potato and sweet potato the night before and then use two pans to poach the eggs. The potato cakes also make a fabulous accompaniment to meat, fish or chicken dishes.

720 g (1 lb 7 oz) potatoes, quartered

420 g (14 oz) orange sweet potato, cut into 3 cm (1 1/4 in) thick slices

2 eggs, lightly whisked

2 tbsp chopped fresh flat-leaf (Italian) parsley

2 tbsp chopped fresh chives

2 1/2 tsp chopped fresh oregano

extra virgin olive oil

2 tbsp white vinegar

8 large eggs, for poaching

300 g (10 oz) baby spinach leaves

SERVES 2 (hearty breakfast)
SERVES 4 (light breakfast)

Potato cake mixture can be made a day ahead and cooked up to 1 hour ahead. Keep warm in the oven as suggested. Eggs can be poached up to 30 minutes ahead. Reheat as outlined in recipe just before serving. Wilt spinach close to serving.

Steam potato and sweet potato for 20 minutes or until tender. Set aside to cool. Pass all potato through a potato ricer fitted with a medium plate into a large bowl. Add eggs, parsley, half the chives and oregano. Season well with salt and pepper and mix until combined.

Heat a large non-stick frying pan over medium heat and brush the pan with oil to lightly grease. Use a 1/3 cup measure to scoop four lots of potato mixture into the pan. Use a spatula to flatten slightly and smooth the top, and cook for 2–3 minutes or until browned underneath. Carefully turn cakes and cook for 2–3 minutes or until browned. Line an oven tray with baking paper. Place potato cakes on tray in oven at 100°C (200°F) to keep warm. Repeat with remaining potato mixture, brushing the pan with oil between batches.

Bring a saucepan of salted water to the boil, add vinegar, then reduce to a gentle simmer. Carefully break 1 egg into a small bowl. Use a wooden spoon to swirl the water in the pan to create a whirlpool. Tip egg into centre of whirlpool and cook for 3–4 minutes or until set on the outside. Use a slotted spoon to lift egg onto a plate lined with paper towel. Continue cooking eggs, placing on the plate when done.

Meanwhile, heat 1 tablespoon oil in a large saucepan over medium heat. Add spinach, cover and cook, tossing leaves occasionally, for 3–4 minutes or until wilted. Season with salt and pepper and set aside.

Carefully lift eggs from plate and return to saucepan of hot water to heat for 1 minute. Lift onto paper towel to drain quickly.

Place potato cakes onto serving plates, top with some spinach and finish with a poached egg. Sprinkle with remaining chives and serve immediately.

GLUTEN-FREE ✔ **DAIRY-FREE** ✔ **DETOX-FRIENDLY** ✔

scrambled eggs

This is our favourite basic scrambled egg recipe. The secret to perfect eggs is to scrape a flat spoon across the base of the pan, as described below, don't stir the eggs. We have added a few variations. Halve the recipe if you would like to serve 2.

8 eggs
³/₄ cup (6 fl oz) soy milk
2 tbsp chopped fresh chives
2 tsp light olive oil
Yeast-free Hi-fibre Bread (page 146),
  to serve

Whisk eggs and milk in a bowl. Stir in chives and season well with salt and pepper.

Heat oil in a frying pan over medium heat. Add egg mixture and cook until the mixture begins to set underneath. Use a flat-tipped wooden spoon to scrape along base of pan from one side to the other to create 'clouds' of cooked egg. Continue drawing the spoon along base of pan until eggs are almost set (the mixture should be a little unset on top).

Spoon onto gluten-free toast to serve.

SERVES 4

Eggs are best cooked just before serving.

VARIATIONS:

* Before cooking the eggs, stir in 100 g (3¹/₂ oz) chopped smoked salmon, 1 tablespoon drained tiny capers and 1 tablespoon finely grated lemon rind. Cook as above but it is unnecessary to season with salt as the salmon and capers are salty.

* Before cooking the eggs, stir in 1 tablespoon chopped fresh parsley, 1 tablespoon chopped fresh basil and 1 teaspoon fresh thyme leaves.

indian-style eggs

This divine breakfast dish is based on a recipe by Ajoy Joshi, from our favourite Indian restaurant in Sydney — Nilgiri's. If you prefer a little more heat, add an extra chilli or serve with a little chopped fresh chilli. A serve of two eggs per person is a hearty breakfast that will keep you going for hours. As part of a brunch meal, however, you can easily serve one egg per person.

2 tbsp light olive oil

2 tsp coriander seeds, lightly crushed

2 brown onions, finely chopped

1 leek, white section thinly sliced

pinch sea salt

1 tbsp finely chopped fresh ginger

2 large cloves garlic, finely chopped

1/2 tsp ground turmeric

800 g (1 lb 10 oz) ripe tomatoes, finely chopped

2 small fresh red chillies, seeded, finely chopped

1/2 cup chopped fresh coriander (cilantro)

8 eggs

Yeast-free Hi-fibre Bread (page 146), to serve

Heat oil in a large frying pan over medium heat. Add coriander seeds and cook for 30 seconds or until fragrant. Add onions, leek and salt and cook, stirring often, for 10 minutes or until golden.

Add ginger, garlic and turmeric and cook, stirring, for 1 minute. Add tomatoes, chillies and 2 tablespoons water, bring to a simmer and cook, stirring occasionally, for 8 minutes or until tomatoes are saucy. Stir in coriander and season well with salt and pepper.

Spread mixture evenly over the base of pan. Make a hollow in the tomato mixture, then break an egg into the hollow. Continue with remaining 7 eggs, spacing them evenly. Cover and cook for 8 minutes for slightly soft yolks or 10 minutes for firm yolks.

Spoon eggs and sauce into serving bowls and serve with gluten-free bread.

SERVES 4–8

The tomato mixture can be made a day ahead and reheated in pan before adding eggs.

GLUTEN-FREE ✔ **DAIRY-FREE** ✔ **DETOX-FRIENDLY** ✔

home-style baked beans

You will never venture into canned baked beans again once you have tried the real thing. In fact, you may want to serve our baked beans for lunch and dinner as well as breakfast. It is a fabulous recipe because you can leave it in the oven and get on with other things while it transforms into a saucy, scrumptious dish. To cook as a detox recipe, reduce the maple syrup to 3 teaspoons.

1 tbsp olive oil

1 large brown onion, chopped

1 large carrot, finely chopped

1 celery stick, finely chopped

1 large red capsicum (pepper), chopped

2 large cloves garlic, finely chopped

1 small fresh red chilli, seeded, finely chopped

375 g (12 oz) dried navy beans (or haricot beans), soaked in cold water overnight, drained

800 g (1 lb 10 oz) can diced tomatoes in juice

1 tbsp gluten-free Dijon mustard

2 bay leaves

4 sprigs fresh thyme

1 tsp ground paprika

2 tbsp pure maple syrup

2 tbsp chopped fresh flat leaf (Italian) parsley

Heat the oil in a flameproof casserole dish over medium heat. Add onion and cook, stirring often, for 10 minutes or until light golden. Add carrot, celery, capsicum, garlic and chilli and cook, stirring occasionally, for 5 minutes.

Add drained beans, tomatoes, mustard, bay leaves, thyme and paprika. Stir in 2^{1}/$_{2}$ cups (20 fl oz) water and bring to the boil. Cover and bake at 160°C (315°F) for 3 hours, stirring the beans after 2 hours and adding extra water if needed, or until beans are tender.

Stir in maple syrup and parsley and season well with salt and pepper.

SERVES 8

Beans can be made up to 2 days ahead. Beans can be frozen in smaller quantities for up to 2 months. Thaw in refrigerator as needed and reheat on the stove.

GLUTEN-FREE ✔   DAIRY-FREE ✔

quinoa & rice porridge
with linseeds & dried vine fruit

If you can't eat oats, here's a delicious alternative to classical porridge.

½ cup (1¾ oz) quinoa flakes

½ cup (2 oz) rolled brown rice flakes

2 tbsp sultanas

2 tbsp currants

1 tbsp linseeds (flax seeds)

brown sugar, to serve

soy or rice milk, to serve

Combine quinoa, rice flakes, sultanas, currants, linseeds and 2 cups (16 fl oz) water in a medium saucepan. Bring to the boil over medium heat. Reduce heat to low and cook, covered, stirring often, for 3 minutes or until mixture reaches a porridge consistency.

Spoon into serving bowls and sprinkle with a little brown sugar. Serve with the milk.

SERVES 2

Porridge is best made close to serving.

french toast with fruit compote

This is a wonderful recipe for French toast for people who can't eat gluten. You can use our Yeast-free Hi-fibre Bread (page 146), which is also gluten-free, or buy an uncut loaf of gluten-free bread if you prefer. If you can't find wild figs, use chopped dried figs. The fruit compote can be served warm or cold.

4 eggs

1 cup (8 fl oz) soy or rice milk

1 tbsp pure maple syrup

8 slices of 1.5 cm (5/8 in) thick
   gluten-free bread

macadamia oil

DRIED FRUIT COMPOTE

1 1/3 cup (10 1/2 fl oz) unsweetened
   100% apple juice

1 cup (1 3/4 oz) halved preservative-free
   dried apple slices

1/2 cup (2 1/2 oz) halved dried wild figs

1/2 cup (2 1/2 oz) sultanas

1/2 cup (1 3/4 oz) raisins

3 cm (1 1/4 in) piece cinnamon stick

To make Dried Fruit Compote, place apple juice, apples, figs, sultanas, raisins and cinnamon in a saucepan. Bring to a simmer over medium heat. Reduce heat to low, cover and cook, stirring gently occasionally, for 15 minutes or until fruit is plump and tender. Set aside to cool.

Whisk together eggs, milk and maple syrup in a bowl until combined. Place bread slices in a shallow dish in a single layer and pour egg mixture over the top. Carefully turn bread to coat in the egg mixture. Set aside for 10 minutes or until all egg mixture has soaked into the bread.

Heat a large non-stick frying pan over medium-high heat. Brush with oil to lightly grease. Add enough bread slices to fit comfortably in the pan and cook for 2 minutes or until golden underneath. Carefully turn the slices and cook for 2 minutes or until golden. Line an oven tray with baking paper and place bread on tray in oven at 100°C (200°F) to keep warm. Repeat with remaining bread slices, brushing the pan with oil before cooking.

Place the toast onto serving plates and serve warm with the fruit compote.

SERVES 4

Dried Fruit Compote will keep, covered, in refrigerator for up to 1 week. French toast can be cooked 1 hour ahead. Keep warm in oven, as suggested.

GLUTEN-FREE ✔ DAIRY-FREE ✔ DETOX-FRIENDLY ✔

apple breakfast muffins

For people in a rush in the morning, our breakfast muffins provide a well-balanced meal that will give you sustained energy throughout the morning. We used unflavoured soy protein powder, or you could use whey protein or rice protein powder if you prefer. Buy these from health food stores. You can also bake the mixture in small $^1/3$ cup ($2^1/2$ fl oz) muffin pans which will take about 25 minutes to cook.

macadamia or light olive oil, to grease

3 cups (15 oz) gluten-free all-purpose
   flour pre-mix

$^1/3$ cup (1$^1/4$ oz) protein powder

1$^1/2$ tbsp gluten-free baking powder

3 tsp ground cinnamon

$^1/2$ tsp ground cardamom

$^1/2$ cup firmly packed (3$^1/2$ oz)
   brown sugar

2 red apples, peeled, cored,
   finely chopped

1 cup (5 oz) currants

$^1/4$ cup (1$^1/2$ oz) sunflower seeds

$^1/4$ cup (1$^1/2$ oz) linseeds (flax seeds)

3 eggs

1$^1/2$ cups (12 fl oz) light soy milk
   or rice milk

100 ml (3$^1/2$ fl oz) macadamia
   or light olive oil

140 g (4$^1/2$ oz) container apple puree

Brush 12 x $^2/3$ -cup (5 fl oz) muffin pans with oil to lightly grease.

Sift flour, protein powder, baking powder, cinnamon and cardamom into a large bowl. Add sugar, apples, currants and seeds and mix well.

Whisk eggs, milk, oil and apple puree together in a separate bowl. Add to dry ingredients and mix with a large spoon until just combined.

Spoon mixture into muffin pans and bake at 180°C (350°F), swapping around after 20 minutes, for 30–32 minutes or until lightly browned and cooked when tested with a skewer (the skewer will be a little sticky). Set aside to cool in pans for a few minutes then transfer to a wire rack to cool completely.

MAKES 12

Muffins will keep in an airtight container for up to 2 days. Freeze, wrapped individually for up to 2 months. Thaw in refrigerator. Can be warmed in oven.

GLUTEN-FREE ✓ DAIRY-FREE ✓

protein powder & berry smoothie

Use your favourite protein powder in this recipe aiming for about 20 g of pure protein (check the nutrition information on the product) – the amount you use will depend on the product. We have given two options for fruit, but you can use any soft seasonal fruit such as mango, custard apple, persimmon and all other berries.

250ml soy or rice milk

2-3 tbsp protein powder, approximately

⅓ cup fresh or frozen blueberries

Place the ingredients in a jug and use a hand-held blender to combine. Or mix in a blender.

VARIATIONS:

In place of blueberries, use 1 small ripe banana and the pulp of 1 to 2 passionfruit.

Add 3 tsp freshly ground linseeds and 1 tsp psyllium husks before blending for a healthy dose of omega-3 fatty acids and increased dietary fibre. Serve immediately as these additions will thicken the drink on standing.

lunch

KATHY: I love lunch and I get quite excited about it. During the week I keep it pretty simple. If I'm working at home I have a salad, like the Roasted Vegetable & Lentil Salad (page 176), or our Leafy Green Salad (page 176), with some Hummus (page 177) and vegetables added. When I am working at Manna from Heaven, we cook a staff lunch every day and it's pot luck. If it's pasta and I am detoxing, I always have a can of tuna on hand and I make a salad. On the days when I'm out and about, I usually lean towards Asian food, maybe a soup or a stir-fry with tofu. On the weekend, it's a different matter. Because I love to cook so much, I take the time to make something a little more elaborate, usually with seafood. I often prepare dishes on the weekend that I can eat during the coming week, such as the Warm Pumpkin, Beetroot & Chickpea Salad with Tahini Sauce (page 78).

JAN: I almost always take my own lunch when I'm working at my clinic (I think home-prepared food always tastes so much better and is much easier because I prefer to avoid gluten and dairy). Lunch is always a protein of some kind with vegetables or salad and sometimes rice or noodles or gluten-free bread. Often I take leftovers from the night before. If I need to buy lunch, I might get a salad and have a protein powder drink or get some fresh rice paper rolls and a salad. On weekends, lunch might be an open sandwich with salad and our Hummus (page 177) or maybe a yummy egg spread that Gavin makes, soup with bread or our Roasted Vegetable & Lentil Salad (page 176). Depends on the season, the mood and what's on.

Whether you are planning a long, lazy weekend lunch or wanting something fast and simple to prepare during a busy week, you will find recipes here to suit you.

We suggest you buy your dry goods on a weekly basis, but shop for fresh ingredients daily if you have the time. If you cook with the seasons, you will be rewarded with flavours at their best. We buy organic or free-range produce and shop at growers' markets, if possible. You meet some remarkable characters, you learn a lot about what you are eating, and it's wonderful to develop a relationship with the farmer.

There is a cross-section of recipes here, with tastes from around the world, using fresh herbs and spices liberally, to give you a full-flavoured experience.

Many of these dishes can be prepared in advance and are ideal to pack for a working lunch. If you have to buy your lunch and have allergies or sensitivities, it can be difficult to buy prepared meals or salads that are free of suspect foods. Remember you can always buy salad ingredients accompanied by some sort of protein such as chicken, salmon, boiled egg or meat from places that sell sandwiches. Ask them to fill a takeaway container with a good selection and perhaps take your own gluten-free bread or some of our Big Rice Salad (page 175).

If you are entertaining, many of the dishes in this section can be served as an entree.

chicken, leek & potato soup with peas

Poached chicken is one of our favourite foods because it is very versatile and the flavours are so pure. You will have some chicken left over from this recipe, which you can use in a salad, such as Asian-style Chicken & Crab Salad with Pink Grapefruit (page 41), or simply make delicious chicken sandwiches. This satisfying soup is also great as a main course, but you will need to increase the quantity.

1.5 kg (3 lb) chicken

1 carrot, coarsely chopped

1 onion, halved

6 black peppercorns

4 stalks fresh parsley

1 tbsp olive oil

1 leek, trimmed and chopped

500 g (1 lb) Sebago potatoes, chopped
   into 2 cm (¾ in) pieces

200 g (6½ oz) peas, podded

1 tbsp small fresh mint leaves

extra virgin olive oil, to serve

Yeast-free Hi-fibre Bread (page 146),
   to serve

Rinse chicken with cold water, then place in a stockpot and cover with water. Add carrot, onion, peppercorns and parsley stalks and bring slowly to the boil, skimming scum from surface, then simmer over low heat for 30 minutes. Turn off heat and cool chicken in pot for 30 minutes. Remove chicken and strain stock. Cool stock and remove fat from surface. You will need 1.5 litres (48 fl oz) stock. Reserve remaining stock for another use.

Halve chicken and reserve one half for another use. Remove skin and bones from remaining chicken and tear meat into bite-sized pieces.

Heat oil in a large saucepan and cook leek, covered, over low heat until soft, adding a little water if sticking to pan. Add potatoes, peas and the 6 cups (48 fl oz) of stock, bring to the boil, then cook over medium heat for about 20 minutes or until potatoes and peas are tender. Add chicken to pan, season to taste and cook over low heat until chicken is warm.

Sprinkle soup with mint leaves, drizzle with extra virgin olive oil and serve with the bread.

SERVES 4

Soup can be prepared a day ahead.

GLUTEN-FREE ✔   **DAIRY-FREE** ✔   DETOX-FRIENDLY ✔   LUNCH BOX ✔

herbed polenta with sautéed chicken livers

If you are on a detox and you want to make this dish, simply leave out the brandy. If you fancy adding a little sweetness to the chicken livers, stir a teaspoon of quince paste into the pan with the stock.

1 tbsp olive oil

1 eschalot (French shallot), finely chopped

1 clove garlic, chopped

1 tsp fresh thyme leaves

400 g (13 oz) chicken livers, trimmed

1 tbsp brandy

2 tbsp Chicken Stock (page 174)

wilted spinach, to serve

HERBED POLENTA

800 ml (26 fl oz) Chicken Stock (page 174) or water

150 g (5 oz) polenta (yellow cornmeal)

pinch cayenne pepper, or to taste

1/4 cup chopped mixed fresh herbs, including basil, mint, flat-leaf (Italian) parsley and dill

olive oil

To make Herbed Polenta, bring stock or water to the boil, add salt to taste, reduce heat and whisk in polenta in a thin stream, stirring well with the whisk. Reduce heat to very low and cook for about 20 minutes, stirring occasionally until all lumps are gone and polenta is thick and comes away from side of pan. Stir in cayenne and herbs and remove from heat. Line an oven tray with baking paper, spoon polenta onto tray and smooth surface. When cool, cut into triangles, return to tray and set aside.

Heat oil in a non-stick frying pan and cook eschalot, garlic and thyme over medium heat for 1 minute. Increase heat to high, add chicken livers and cook until browned. Flambé with brandy, season to taste, then add stock and bring to the boil. Remove from heat.

Brush polenta with oil and place under a hot grill (broiler) until golden, then turn and cook other side.

Serve polenta topped with wilted spinach and chicken liver mixture.

SERVES 4

Polenta can be prepared a day ahead.

chicken, pork & veal terrine with beetroot salsa

The rich flavours of this terrine are perfectly complemented by the freshness of the beetroot salsa. You could also serve it with roasted witlof or asparagus, or try it with Baby Spinach & Pomegranate Seed Salad (page 176). It's great to take on picnics. Minced pork and chicken can sometimes be fatty, so give your butcher a few days notice and ask him to mince lean meat for you.

10 slices prosciutto, trimmed of fat

250 g (8 oz) lean minced (ground) pork

250 g (8 oz) lean minced (ground) chicken

2 tbsp shelled pistachios, peeled

1 egg, lightly beaten

good pinch ground allspice

1 lemon, peeled, segmented and coarsely chopped

2 large eschalots (French shallots), finely chopped

2 tbsp chopped fresh chives

2 chicken thigh fillets, trimmed of fat

160 g (5 oz) veal escalopes

rocket (arugula) leaves and Olive & Thyme Focaccia (page 148), to serve

BEETROOT SALSA

3 large beetroot (beets), trimmed

2 tbsp olive oil

1 tbsp balsamic vinegar

2 tbsp chopped fresh chives

To make Beetroot Salsa, wrap beetroot in foil, place on an oven tray and roast at 200°C (400°F) for 45–60 minutes or until beetroot are tender. Remove foil and, when cool enough to handle, peel away skin. Cut beetroot into 1 cm ($1/2$ in) dice, combine with remaining salsa ingredients and season to taste.

Line a 1.5-litre (48 fl oz) capacity loaf pan with two-thirds of the prosciutto, leaving it to overhang the sides of the pan.

Combine minced pork, minced chicken, pistachios, egg, allspice, lemon, eschalots and chives and season liberally to taste. Place half the minced meat mixture in base of pan, top with chicken, veal and remaining mince mixture. Place remaining prosciutto slices on top and then fold overhanging prosciutto over. Cover with a double layer of foil, place in a roasting pan and pour in enough hot water to come halfway up sides of the loaf pan. Bake at 180°C (350°F) for 1 hour or until meat juices run clear.

Remove terrine from oven and place a weight on it while it cools. Remove from loaf pan and scrape away jelly from around terrine. Cover and refrigerate. Serve sliced with Beetroot Salsa, rocket leaves and focaccia.

SERVES 8 (entree)
SERVES 4–6 (lunch)

Terrine can be prepared a day ahead.

GLUTEN-FREE ✔   DAIRY-FREE ✔   LUNCH BOX ✔

marinated quail with red cabbage salad

If you have time, prepare the quails the day before and leave them to marinate overnight, as this will really enhance the flavours. Don't be put off the recipe if you don't have the luxury of time – they are still delicious with only 30 minutes of marinating. If you can't get quail, use chicken thigh fillets or trimmed duck breasts.

4 large quail

250 g (8 oz) red cabbage,
  thinly shredded

150 g (5 oz) Chinese cabbage,
  thinly shredded

1 tsp salt

2 tbsp toasted sesame seeds

4 green (spring) onions (scallions), sliced
  on the diagonal

1 large fresh green chilli, sliced

1/2 cup firmly packed torn fresh mint
  leaves

freshly ground black pepper

vegetable oil

lime wedges, to serve

MARINADE

1/4 cup (2 fl oz) wheat-free tamari sauce

2 tsp five-spice powder

1 cinnamon stick

2 cloves garlic, sliced

2 cm (3/4 in) piece fresh ginger, sliced

2 tsp sugar

juice of 1 lime

To make Marinade, combine all ingredients.

Cut quail in half down either side of backbone and discard backbone. Cut in half through breastbone. Place quail, skin-side up, on a cooking rack over a roasting pan and pour boiling water over the quail. Transfer quail to a bowl and pour marinade over. Cover and marinate for 5 hours or overnight in refrigerator.

Place both cabbages in a bowl, add the salt, toss to combine and stand for 30 minutes. Combine cabbage, sesame seeds, green onions, chilli and mint and season with black pepper.

Drain quail and reserve marinade. Brush quail with oil, brown in a non-stick frying pan and place on an oven tray. Roast at 200°C (400°F) for 10 minutes, then rest, loosely covered, in a warm place for 10 minutes. Place strained marinade ingredients in a saucepan, add any juices from quail and simmer over low heat for 2 minutes.

Top cabbage salad with quail and drizzle with marinade. Serve with wedges of lime.

SERVES 4

Quail and salad can be prepared a day ahead.

GLUTEN-FREE ✔   DAIRY-FREE ✔   DETOX-FRIENDLY ✔   LUNCH BOX ✔

asian-style chicken & crab salad with pink grapefruit

Surprisingly, combining poultry and seafood in the one dish really does work. If you prefer, leave the crab out and add a little more chicken (or leave the chicken out and add more crab meat). For a more substantial meal, serve on a bed of rice noodles.

2 skinless chicken breast fillets

1 bunch asparagus, trimmed, halved
    lengthwise

100 g (3 1/2 oz) snowpeas (mangetout),
    cut into julienne

1 carrot, cut into julienne

200 g (6 1/2 oz) crab meat

1 Lebanese (small green) cucumber,
    peeled, seeded, cut into julienne

1 pink grapefruit, peeled, segmented

1/4 cup firmly packed fresh Vietnamese
    mint leaves

2 tbsp vegetable oil

2 eschalots (French shallots), thinly sliced

DRESSING

2 tbsp fish sauce

1 tbsp lime juice

1 small fresh red chilli, seeded, finely
    chopped

1 clove garlic, finely chopped

1/2 tsp caster (superfine) sugar

To make Dressing, combine all ingredients and season to taste.

Place chicken in a shallow frying pan and cover with water. Bring slowly to the boil and turn off heat. Turn chicken over and stand in water for 10 minutes or until chicken is cooked. Remove and cool, then tear chicken into bite-sized pieces.

Place asparagus, snowpeas and carrot in a bowl, pour boiling water over, then drain and rinse under cold water. Place in a serving bowl and add chicken, crab, cucumber, grapefruit and mint. Pour the dressing over and toss gently to combine.

Heat oil in a small saucepan and cook eschalots over medium heat until crisp and golden, then drain on paper towel. Serve salad topped with eschalots.

SERVES 4

Chicken can be poached a day ahead.

cos salad with mustard chicken & soft-boiled eggs

This is an ideal salad to serve on a large platter and place in the centre of the table for family and friends to help themselves. This casual way of eating is becoming more popular and means less stress in the kitchen. Use chicken breast fillets if you need to lower your cholesterol, but we think chicken thighs have more flavour.

4 large chicken thigh fillets, trimmed of fat

4 slices prosciutto

olive oil

6 eggs

1 cos (romaine) lettuce, outer leaves removed

100 g (3 1/2 oz) cherry tomatoes, halved

6 green (spring) onions (scallions), chopped

sea salt

MUSTARD DRESSING

2 tsp gluten-free seeded mustard

1 tbsp red wine vinegar

2 tbsp extra virgin olive oil

1 tbsp chopped fresh chives

To make Mustard Dressing, combine all ingredients and season to taste.

Wrap chicken fillets in prosciutto and brush with oil. Cook in a non-stick frying pan over high heat until browned on both sides. Remove and place on an oven tray and roast at 200°C (400°F) for 10–15 minutes, depending on thickness. Remove from oven and cool to room temperature, then slice on the diagonal.

Bring water to the boil in a saucepan, carefully add eggs and cook, simmering gently for 5 minutes. Remove eggs and plunge into cold water for 5 minutes. Carefully peel eggs and slice in half.

Remove leaves from lettuce and place on a large platter. Pile cherry tomatoes in the centre of plate, place sliced chicken on top, then drizzle chicken and lettuce with Mustard Dressing. Place eggs around chicken and sprinkle with green onions and sea salt.

SERVES 4

Best made just before serving.

GLUTEN-FREE ✔   DAIRY-FREE ✔   DETOX-FRIENDLY ✔   LUNCH BOX ✔

radicchio & thyme risotto with flattened chicken

Radicchio is a wonderful bitter leaf and works as well in a risotto as it does in a salad. This is a simple risotto, but that's what makes it so special – you can taste all the components, which are in perfect balance. The risotto also goes well with lamb or can be eaten on its own, with the addition of some toasted pinenuts. One of Peter Snowball's favourites!

4 chicken thigh fillets, trimmed of fat
olive oil
1 tsp fresh thyme leaves
sprigs fresh thyme and lemon wedges,
  to serve

RADICCHIO & THYME RISOTTO

1 tbsp olive oil
1 red (Spanish) onion, chopped
150 g (5 oz) radicchio leaves, shredded
2 cloves garlic, chopped
1 cup (6 1/2 oz) arborio rice
1 litre (32 fl oz) Chicken Stock
  (page 174), approximately
1 tsp fresh thyme leaves

To make Radicchio & Thyme Risotto, heat oil in a large saucepan and cook onion, covered, over low heat until soft. Add radicchio and garlic and stir until radicchio is wilted. Add rice and stir over medium heat until rice is coated. Have stock simmering in another saucepan. Add 1 cup (8 fl oz) stock to the rice and stir over heat until stock is absorbed. Add remaining stock 1/2 cup (4 fl oz) at a time, stirring constantly, and allowing each addition to be absorbed before adding the next. With the last addition of stock, add thyme. Remove from heat, cover and stand for 5 minutes.

Meanwhile, pound chicken with the flat side of a meat mallet or rolling pin until about 1 cm (1/2 in) thick. Brush chicken with oil, sprinkle with thyme and season to taste. Chargrill chicken on both sides until brown and cooked. Rest, loosely covered, in a warm place for 5 minutes.

Serve Radicchio & Thyme Risotto on a flat plate topped with chicken and sprigs of thyme, with lemon wedges to one side.

SERVES 4

Best made just before serving.

GLUTEN-FREE ✔   DAIRY-FREE ✔   DETOX-FRIENDLY ✔

mediterranean-style quinoa & chicken dumpling soup

This light tangy soup, suitable for both winter and summer, can be eaten either hot or at room temperature. The addition of quinoa (an ancient South American grain high in protein) to the soup gives it body and texture.

3 litres (96 fl oz) Chicken Stock (page 174)

2 cinnamon sticks

4 cardamom pods, crushed

1 cup (3½ oz) quinoa

1 tbsp coarsely chopped fresh flat-leaf (Italian) parsley

1 tbsp coarsely chopped fresh mint

¼ cup (2 fl oz) lemon juice

Olive & Thyme Focaccia (page 148), to serve

CHICKEN DUMPLINGS

4 cardamom pods

½ tsp toasted cumin seeds

400 g (13 oz) lean minced (ground) chicken

¼ cup (1 oz) chickpea (besan) flour

2 cloves garlic, crushed

1 tbsp chopped fresh flat-leaf (Italian) parsley

2 eggs, lightly beaten

Put stock, cinnamon and cardamom in a large saucepan and bring to the boil over medium heat. Reduce liquid to 2 litres (64 fl oz). Remove cinnamon and cardamom. Add quinoa and simmer for a further 15 minutes, then season to taste.

To make Chicken Dumplings, remove seeds from cardamom pods, place in a mortar with the cumin seeds and crush with a pestle. Combine crushed spices, minced chicken, chickpea flour, garlic, parsley and eggs in a food processor, season to taste and process until mixture comes together. Using wet hands, shape mixture into walnut-sized balls.

Add dumplings to gently simmering stock mixture and simmer for 2 minutes. Just before serving, stir in parsley, mint and lemon juice. Serve with focaccia.

SERVES 4

Makes about 20 dumplings

Soup can be prepared a day ahead.

venison fillets with moroccan date salad

The slightly gamey flavour of venison marries beautifully with the sweetness of the dates and oranges in this salad. This is a perfect lunch on its own but if you want a more substantial meal, serve it with Big Rice Salad (page 175) or Roasted Vegetable & Lentil Salad (page 176).

2 X 300 g (10 oz) fillets of venison

olive oil

2 cups firmly packed watercress leaves

Yeast-free Hi-fibre Bread (page 146),
   toasted, to serve

Roasted Garlic Puree (page 176),
   to serve

DATE SALAD

4 blood oranges, peeled, sliced

4 radishes, trimmed, thinly sliced on a
   mandolin

1 small red (Spanish) onion, halved,
   thinly sliced

10 fresh dates, pitted and coarsely
   chopped

¼ cup (1 ½ oz) baby black olives

¼ cup firmly packed fresh mint leaves

2 tbsp lemon juice

2 tbsp extra virgin olive oil

2 tbsp toasted flaked almonds

Rub venison with oil and cook over high heat in a non-stick frying pan until browned all over. Place on an oven tray and roast at 200°C (400°F) for 15 minutes. Remove from oven and rest, loosely covered, in a warm place for 10 minutes.

To make Date Salad, place orange slices in a large flat bowl, add radishes and toss gently. Top with onion, dates, olives and mint leaves. Combine lemon juice and oil and season to taste. Drizzle dressing over the salad. Just before serving sprinkle with almonds.

Place sliced venison on a bed of watercress with the Date Salad to one side. Serve with toasted bread topped with Roasted Garlic Puree.

SERVES 4

Best made before serving.

aromatic beef soup with star anise

This Vietnamese-style soup is sometimes called 'pho' and is a very satisfying soup for lunch. To make the beef easier to slice, partially freeze it first, then use a sharp thin-bladed knife. You can also substitute the beef with thinly sliced chicken breasts.

1.5 litres (48 fl oz) Chicken Stock (page 174)

2.5 cm (1 in) piece fresh ginger, peeled, coarsely chopped

1 star anise

1 cinnamon stick

1 onion, halved

2 cloves garlic, halved

1 tbsp chopped lemongrass

1 tbsp fish sauce

400 g (13 oz) beef fillet, very thinly sliced

250 g (8 oz) fresh rice noodles

100 g (3½ oz) bean sprouts, trimmed

2 small fresh red chillies, thinly sliced

3 green (spring) onions (scallions), thinly sliced

1 tbsp chopped fresh coriander (cilantro) leaves

1 tbsp chopped fresh mint leaves

lime wedges, to serve

CHILLI SAUCE

3 large fresh red chillies, chopped

juice of 1 lime, or to taste

2 cloves garlic, chopped

pinch sugar, to taste

sea salt

To make Chilli Sauce, combine all ingredients in the small bowl of a food processor and process until smooth. Season to taste with sea salt.

Combine stock, ginger, star anise, cinnamon, onion, garlic, lemongrass and fish sauce in a saucepan and gradually bring to the boil. Simmer over medium heat for 10 minutes, then strain. Return stock to pan and reheat. Just before serving, add beef and turn off heat.

Meanwhile, cook noodles according to directions on packet, then place in deep bowls. Spoon stock and beef mixture over noodles and top with bean sprouts, chillies, green onions, coriander and mint. Serve with lime wedges and Chilli Sauce.

SERVES 4

Chilli sauce and stock mixture can be prepared a day ahead.

GLUTEN-FREE ✔   DAIRY-FREE ✔   DETOX-FRIENDLY ✔

spiced rare beef with roasted sweet potato & split pea sauce

Roasted sweet potato is one of Kathy's favourites – she likes to cook it until the edges are almost burnt, caramelised and scrumptious. We also use this split pea sauce as a spread for toasted gluten-free bread or as a dip with crudités.

1 tsp black peppercorns

1 tsp coriander seeds, coarsely ground

1/2 tsp smoked paprika

1 tsp salt

600 g (1 lb 3 oz) piece sirloin steak, trimmed of fat

olive oil

400 g (13 oz) orange sweet potato, cut into 1–2 cm (1/2 – 3/4 in) pieces

2 cups rocket (arugula) leaves

1 tbsp lemon juice

SPLIT PEA SAUCE

1 cup (6 1/2 oz) yellow split peas

1 head garlic

2 tbsp lemon juice

1 tbsp olive oil

To make Split Pea Sauce, cook split peas in simmering water for about 35 minutes or until very soft. Drain.

Place whole garlic head on an oven tray and bake at 200°C (400°F) for 30 minutes or until tender. When cool enough to handle, squeeze garlic from cloves. Combine garlic, split peas, lemon juice and oil in a food processor, season to taste and process until smooth.

Combine black peppercorns, coriander, paprika and salt in a spice grinder and process until smooth, or crush using a mortar and pestle. Rub beef with 1 tablespoon oil, then rub in three-quarters of the spice mix. Cover and refrigerate for 2 hours.

Heat a little more oil in a non-stick frying pan and cook beef over high heat on all sides until well browned. Place on an oven tray and roast at 200°C (400°F) for 15 minutes for very rare. Rest, loosely covered, in a warm place for 10 minutes, then slice paper thin.

Toss sweet potato with a little oil, place on an oven tray and roast at 200°C (400°F), turning occasionally, for 30 minutes or until golden.

Toss rocket with lemon juice and 1 tablespoon oil and season to taste.

Spoon a little Split Pea Sauce onto plates, top with rocket, sweet potato and sliced beef, then sprinkle with remaining spice mix. Serve any remaining sauce separately.

SERVES 4

Split pea sauce can be made a day ahead.

sumac-spiced lamb backstraps with quinoa & roasted grapes

Roasted grapes work wonderfully with a range of dishes: cook them just until their skins burst and they form a delicious sauce. We have served this dish as a main course for dinner, using wilted spinach instead of baby spinach leaves. Also good with duck and quail.

600 g (1 lb 3 oz) lamb backstraps (eye of loin)

olive oil

1 tbsp sumac

1 tbsp fresh lemon thyme leaves

1 tsp freshly ground black pepper

400 g (13 oz) seedless black grapes

1 cup baby spinach leaves

lemon wedges, to serve

QUINOA SALAD

1 cup (6¼ oz) quinoa

2 cups (16 fl oz) Chicken Stock (page 174)

½ preserved lemon, skin only, chopped

2 cloves garlic, chopped

4 green (spring) onions (scallions), finely chopped

1 tbsp fresh lemon thyme leaves

1 tbsp chopped fresh oregano

1 tbsp extra virgin olive oil

To make Quinoa Salad, combine quinoa and stock in a saucepan, season with salt and bring to the boil over high heat. Reduce heat to low and simmer, covered, for about 15 minutes or until stock is absorbed and quinoa is tender. Remove lid and stir over low heat until all liquid has evaporated. Remove from heat and cool to room temperature, then stir in remaining ingredients.

Brush lamb with a little oil and rub with sumac, thyme and black pepper. Fry lamb in a non-stick frying pan until browned, then place on an oven tray. Toss grapes with a little oil and place beside lamb. Roast at 200°C (400°F) for about 10 minutes for pink lamb. Remove lamb and rest, loosely covered, in a warm place for 10 minutes, then slice on the diagonal. Meanwhile, return grapes to oven and roast for another 10 minutes or until just beginning to burst.

Top baby spinach leaves with Quinoa Salad and sliced lamb, spoon grapes and their juices over and serve with lemon wedges.

SERVES 4

Quinoa salad can be prepared a day ahead.

GLUTEN-FREE ✔ DAIRY-FREE ✔ DETOX-FRIENDLY ✔ LUNCH BOX ✔

grilled kofta with pomegranate & parsley salad

Pomegranate seeds are bursting with flavour and make a wonderful addition to salads. Remember to wear an apron when you remove the seeds, as the colour is so vibrant it can stain your clothes if splashed. You can vary the size of the kofta: walnut-sized kofta can be served as an appetiser topped with Hummus (page 177) or you can make them burger-sized.

olive oil

Coriander & Chilli Corn Bread
  (page 145), toasted, to serve

LAMB KOFTA

400 g (13 oz) lean minced (ground)
  lamb

1/2 cup (1 3/4 oz) long-grain rice, cooked

1 egg, lightly whisked

1/2 onion, finely chopped

1 tsp finely chopped fresh dill

1 tsp finely chopped fresh flat-leaf
  (Italian) parsley

pinch ground cinnamon

POMEGRANATE & PARSLEY SALAD

1 pomegranate, halved

1/2 red (Spanish) onion, finely chopped

2 tbsp coarsely chopped toasted
  hazelnuts

2 cups firmly packed fresh flat-leaf
  (Italian) parsley leaves

2 tsp pomegranate molasses

2 tbsp extra virgin olive oil

To make Lamb Kofta, combine lamb and remaining ingredients in a bowl and season to taste. Use a 1/4-cup measure to scoop 8 lots of mixture and form into round balls or patties. Place on an oven tray and brush with oil. Grill (broil) kofta until golden, then turn and grill other side.

To make Pomegranate & Parsley Salad, remove seeds from pomegranate using a teaspoon and place in a bowl. Add remaining ingredients, season to taste and toss gently.

Serve toasted corn bread with Pomegranate & Parsley Salad topped with grilled kofta.

SERVES 4

Lamb kofta can be prepared a day ahead.
Photograph appears on front cover.

GLUTEN-FREE ✓　**DAIRY-FREE** ✓　**DETOX-FRIENDLY** ✓　**LUNCH BOX** ✓

open steak sandwich with caramelised onions

This recipe is full of great flavours – garlicky mayonnaise, caramelised onions and roasted beetroot – and is quick and simple to make. You can substitute Hummus (page 177) for the Aioli if you like. That's what Jan would do, but Kathy has a real weakness for any kind of mayonnaise. Thin sirloin steaks or venison steaks are also suitable for this recipe.

2 beetroot (beets), trimmed

olive oil

2 red (Spanish) onions, halved, sliced

1 tbsp balsamic vinegar

1 tsp brown sugar

4 X 100 g (3½ oz) scotch fillet steaks

1 quantity Aioli (page 177)

1 tsp gluten-free seeded mustard

4 thick slices Yeast-free Hi-fibre Bread (page 146), toasted

1 avocado, sliced

1 small oak leaf lettuce, leaves separated

Wrap beetroot in foil, place on an oven tray and roast at 200°C (400°F) for 45 minutes or until tender. Cool, then rub off skins and slice.

Heat 1 tablespoon oil in a saucepan and cook onions, covered, over very low heat for about 20 minutes or until soft, adding a little water if onions are sticking to pan. Remove lid, add vinegar and sugar and stir over heat until onions are caramelised.

Brush steaks with oil and season to taste. Cook on a chargrill over high heat for about 60 seconds each side.

Combine Aioli and mustard, spread over toasted bread and place on plates. Top with avocado, beetroot, lettuce leaves and steaks. Spoon onion over steaks and serve immediately.

SERVES 4

Best made just before serving.

steamed cuttlefish & prawns with vietnamese-style coleslaw

Cuttlefish is messy to clean, so ask your fishmonger to clean it for you. It is inexpensive and sadly underutilised – if you haven't used it before, give it a try. You can double the quantity of cuttlefish and leave out the prawns if you like, and if you can't find cuttlefish, use squid instead.

2 X 500 g (1 lb) cuttlefish, cleaned

12 medium green prawns (shrimp), peeled and deveined, tails intact

1 carrot, cut into julienne

300 g (10 oz) Chinese cabbage, finely shredded

3 green (spring) onions (scallions), trimmed and sliced on the diagonal

50 g (1 3/4 oz) snowpea (mangetout) sprouts, trimmed

12 cherry tomatoes, halved

1/4 cup firmly packed fresh coriander (cilantro) leaves

35 g (1 1/4 oz) toasted chopped peanuts or cashews

SWEET CHILLI SAUCE

2 tbsp rice vinegar

1 tbsp caster (superfine) sugar

2 large fresh red chillies, seeded, chopped

To make Sweet Chilli Sauce, combine all ingredients in a saucepan, add 1/4 cup (2 fl oz) water and simmer over low heat for about 10 minutes or until syrupy. Cool.

Slice cuttlefish into 2 mm (1/16 in) thick slices. Cook cuttlefish and prawns in batches in the top of a double steamer over a pan of simmering water for about 1 minute for the cuttlefish and 1–2 minutes for the prawns, or until just cooked.

Place carrot in a bowl, cover with boiling water, then drain and rinse under cold water.

Combine cuttlefish, prawns and carrot with remaining ingredients, toss with sweet chilli sauce and serve immediately.

SERVES 4

Sweet chilli sauce can be prepared a day ahead.

GLUTEN-FREE ✔ **DAIRY-FREE** ✔ **DETOX-FRIENDLY** ✔ **LUNCH BOX** ✔

green mango, lemongrass & pork salad

If you are allergic to chilli, leave it out of the recipe – the salad is still delicious without it. If palm sugar is unavailable, brown sugar can be used instead.

400 g (13 oz) piece pork fillet, cut into
  1 cm (1/2 in) thick slices

1 tbsp rice flour

1/4 cup (2 fl oz) vegetable oil

1 small green mango, peeled and cut into julienne

1 tbsp finely chopped lemongrass

1 tbsp finely shredded kaffir (makrut) lime leaves

6 eschalots (French shallots), thinly sliced

3 baby bok choy (pak choy), trimmed and
  shredded

200 g (6 1/2 oz) bean sprouts, trimmed

1/4 cup firmly packed fresh Vietnamese mint leaves

1/4 cup firmly packed fresh coriander
  (cilantro) leaves

1/4 cup firmly packed fresh Thai basil leaves

HOT & SOUR SAUCE

2 large fresh red chillies, chopped

4 cloves garlic, chopped

1 tbsp wheat-free tamari sauce

2 tbsp fish sauce

1/4 cup (2 fl oz) lime juice

grated palm sugar (jaggery), to taste

To make the Hot & Sour Sauce, using a mortar and pestle, pound chillies and garlic to form a paste, then whisk in remaining ingredients.

Toss pork with rice flour. Heat oil in a wok and stir-fry pork in batches over high heat until cooked through. Drain on paper towel and cool.

Combine mango and remaining ingredients and toss gently with half the sauce. Top with pork, drizzle with remaining sauce and serve.

SERVES 4

Sauce can be prepared 3 hours ahead.

GLUTEN-FREE ✔ **DAIRY-FREE** ✔ **LUNCH BOX** ✔

moreton bay bug & snake bean salad

Moreton Bay bug meat is a delicacy. If you can't buy the bugs already shelled, you will need to do it yourself. Buy live bugs and place them in a slurry of ice or the freezer. Remove the heads. Using kitchen scissors, cut through the soft underside of the shell on both sides of the meat, peel the shell back and pull the meat out. You can substitute peeled green prawns.

vegetable oil

500 g (1 lb) Moreton Bay bug meat,
  halved lengthwise

3 eschalots (French shallots), sliced

3 cloves garlic, sliced

4 kaffir (makrut) lime leaves, finely
  shredded

3 cm (1 1/4 in) piece fresh ginger, peeled
  and cut into julienne

200 g (6 1/2 oz) snake beans (yard-long
  beans), trimmed and cut into
  4 cm (1 1/2 in) lengths

100 g (3 1/2 oz) sugar snap peas,
  trimmed

100 g (3 1/2 oz) bean sprouts, trimmed

50 g (1 3/4 oz) snowpea sprouts, trimmed

35 g (1 1/4 oz) toasted slivered almonds

DRESSING

1 tbsp fish sauce

1 tsp sesame oil

1 tbsp lime juice

2 tbsp light coconut milk

1 tsp grated palm sugar (jaggery)

To make Dressing, whisk ingredients together and season to taste.

Heat 1 tablespoon oil in a wok and stir-fry bug meat in batches over high heat until just cooked. Remove from wok and place in a bowl.

Add another tablespoon of oil to the wok and stir-fry eschalots, garlic, lime leaves and ginger over high heat for 1 minute, then add to bug meat in bowl and toss gently with half the dressing.

Cook snake beans in simmering salted water for 2 minutes, add sugar snap peas and return to the boil, then drain and rinse under cold water.

Place in a serving bowl, add bean sprouts and snowpea sprouts and toss with remaining dressing, then toss gently with bug meat mixture.

Serve sprinkled with toasted almonds.

SERVES 4

Best made just before serving.

fish soup with capsicum & almond rouille

This is a wonderful robust soup, suitable for all seasons, for either lunch or dinner. If you like strong fishy flavours, use fish stock as the base, but if you prefer a more subtle flavour, use chicken stock. Make sure the mussels and clams have been well degorged and are free of sand.

2 unpeeled desiree potatoes

1 tbsp olive oil

2 onions, chopped

1 tsp sweet paprika

3 cloves garlic, chopped

4 tomatoes, peeled, chopped

½ cup (4 fl oz) white wine or water

400 ml (13 fl oz) Fish Stock or Chicken Stock (page 174)

12 medium green prawns (shrimp), peeled and deveined, tails intact

500 g (1 lb) black mussels, scrubbed and bearded

500 g (1 lb) clams, soaked in cold water for 30 minutes

400 g (13 oz) firm white fish such as ling, cut into 2 cm (¾ in) pieces

Yeast-free Hi-fibre Bread (page 146), toasted, to serve

CAPSICUM & ALMOND ROUILLE

1 red capsicum (pepper)

50 g (1¾ oz) blanched almonds

3 cloves garlic, chopped

¼ cup (2 fl oz) olive oil

To make Capsicum & Almond Rouille, place capsicum on an oven tray and roast at 200°C (400°F) for 30 minutes or until skin is blistered and blackened. Place in a bowl, cover with foil and stand for 10 minutes. Remove skin and seeds. Place almonds on oven tray and roast at 200°C (400°F) for 15 minutes. Combine capsicum and almonds in a food processor with remaining ingredients and process until smooth, then season to taste.

Cook potatoes in simmering salted water until tender. Drain. When cool enough to handle, peel and slice.

Heat oil in a large, heavy-based saucepan, add onions and cook, covered, over low heat until soft, then add paprika and stir for 1 minute. Add garlic and tomatoes and cook over high heat until tomatoes are thick and pulpy. Add white wine or water and stock and simmer for about 5 minutes.

Add seafood to pan, cover tightly with a lid and cook over medium heat for 5–10 minutes or until mussels and clams open. Discard any that do not open. Add potatoes and season to taste, then cover and cook for another 2 minutes or until potato is heated through.

Serve soup topped with a spoonful of Capsicum & Almond Rouille. Serve remaining rouille with toasted gluten-free bread.

SERVES 4–6

Rouille can be made a day ahead.

GLUTEN-FREE ✔ DAIRY-FREE ✔ DETOX-FRIENDLY ✔ LUNCH BOX ✔

stuffed squid with roasted capsicum & rocket salad

You really do need small squid for this recipe. Ask your fishmonger to clean them for you, but make sure you see them first so you know they are fresh. The roasted capsicum and rocket salad is also delicious served with grilled sardines.

12 small squid, about 7–8 cm
 (2¾ in – 3¼ in) long

⅓ cup chopped fresh flat-leaf
 (Italian) parsley

1 tbsp chopped fresh oregano

50 g (1¾ oz) rocket (arugula) leaves,
 shredded

2 tbsp lemon juice

1 tsp freshly ground black pepper,
 or to taste

olive oil

sea salt

8 anchovy fillets, to serve

lemon wedges and Coriander & Chilli
 Corn Bread (page 146), to serve

ROASTED CAPSICUM & ROCKET SALAD

1 red capsicum (pepper), sliced
 lengthwise, 1 cm (½ in) thick

12 cloves garlic

extra virgin olive oil

2 tsp balsamic vinegar

¼ cup (1½ oz) baby black olives

2 cups rocket (arugula) leaves

To make Roasted Capsicum & Rocket Salad, combine capsicum and garlic on an oven tray and toss with 1 tablespoon oil. Roast at 200°C (400°F) for 30 minutes, stirring occasionally, until capsicum is soft and browning on the edges. Season to taste and stir in balsamic vinegar and olives. Toss rocket with a little oil, then toss with capsicum mixture.

Clean squid and reserve tentacles. Rinse under cold water and remove the outer thin, filmy skin, then pat dry with paper towel.

To make stuffing, combine parsley, oregano, rocket and lemon juice and season with pepper. Spoon equal amounts of stuffing into cavity of each squid.

Brush squid and tentacles with oil and cook on both sides on the flat plate of a chargrill or barbecue, or fry in a non-stick frying pan until just changed in colour. Rest squid, loosely covered, in a warm place for 5 minutes, then sprinkle with sea salt.

Place mounds of rocket salad in the middle of each plate and top with 2 anchovy fillets. Scatter stuffed squid and tentacles around, add lemon wedges and serve with corn bread.

SERVES 4

Best made just before serving.

GLUTEN-FREE ✓ DAIRY-FREE ✓ DETOX-FRIENDLY ✓ LUNCH BOX ✓

chargrilled sardines
with celeriac remoulade

Sardines are high in omega 3 fatty acids, which are wonderful anti-inflammatory agents in the body. Not only are omega 3s good for reducing inflammation, they also help to reduce the risk of cardiovascular disease. You could use garfish or red mullet fillets for this recipe.

4 small Roma (plum) tomatoes, halved
   lengthwise
olive oil
16 butterflied sardines
rocket (arugula) leaves and lemon
   wedges, to serve

CELERIAC REMOULADE
¼ cup (2 fl oz) lemon juice
600 g (1 lb 3 oz) celeriac
1 quantity Aioli (page 177)
1 tbsp chopped fresh basil
2 tsp baby capers
4 cornichons, chopped
3 green (spring) onions (scallions),
   chopped

To make Celeriac Remoulade, combine lemon juice and 2 cups (16 fl oz) cold water in a bowl. Peel celeriac and slice thinly with a mandolin, if available. Cut into matchsticks, placing in the acidulated (lemon) water as you go. Combine Aioli and remaining ingredients and check seasoning. Drain celeriac well and stir into Aioli mixture.

Place tomatoes on an oven tray, brush with oil and season to taste. Roast at 120°C (235°F) for 1 hour, then remove from oven and cool to room temperature.

Brush sardines with oil and chargrill or grill (broil) for 1 minute each side or until just cooked.

Serve rocket leaves topped with tomatoes and sardines and place Celeriac Remoulade and lemon wedges to one side.

SERVES 4

Remoulade can be prepared a day ahead.

seared scallop & green mango salad

This pretty salad is ideal to serve as an entree or as a lunch dish. We like to use the large Queensland scallops without roe. Order them in advance so that you get fresh scallops, as they have a much better flavour than frozen ones.

2 green (spring) onions (scallions),
   trimmed and cut into julienne

1 carrot, cut into julienne

100 g (3 1/2 oz) snowpeas (mangetout),
   cut into julienne

50 g (1 3/4 oz) snowpea sprouts, trimmed

1 Lebanese (small green) cucumber,
   peeled, seeded and cut into julienne

1/2 green mango, peeled, cut into
   julienne

1/3 cup firmly packed fresh coriander
   (coriander) leaves

16 scallops, without roe

olive oil

1 small avocado, chopped into 1 cm
   (1/2 in) pieces

DRESSING

1/2 red capsicum (pepper), very finely
   chopped

2 tbsp wheat-free tamari sauce

1/2 tsp brown sugar

2 tbsp olive oil

2 tbsp lime juice

To make Dressing, combine all ingredients and season to taste. Stand for 30 minutes for flavours to develop.

Place green onions in cold water for 30 minutes, then drain. Place carrot and snowpeas in a bowl, cover with boiling water for 30 seconds, then drain and rinse under cold water. Place the drained vegetables in a bowl and add snowpea sprouts, cucumber, green mango and coriander and toss gently.

Brush scallops with a little oil and cook in a very hot frying pan for about 20 seconds each side.

Divide salad among plates, top with avocado and scallops, then spoon dressing over salad and around the plate.

SERVES 4

Dressing can be prepared 3 hours ahead.

GLUTEN-FREE ✔ **DAIRY-FREE** ✔ **DETOX-FRIENDLY** ✔

marinated octopus with parsley & white bean salad

It is really important that you don't overcook octopus, as it will become tough and rubbery. Cook until it just changes in colour, then it will be tender and sweet. Marinating also helps to tenderise octopus.

8 X 600 g (1 lb 3 oz) baby octopus, cleaned, halved

1 tbsp olive oil

2 tbsp lemon juice

1 tsp sweet paprika

pinch cayenne pepper, or to taste

2 cloves garlic, chopped

2 bay leaves

lemon wedges, to serve

PARSLEY & WHITE BEAN SALAD

1 tbsp olive oil

1 red (Spanish) onion, halved, sliced

2 tbsp balsamic vinegar

2 tbsp lemon-pressed olive oil

1/4 cup (1 1/2 oz) black olives, pitted, sliced

1 cup firmly packed fresh flat-leaf (Italian) parsley leaves

2 x 400 g (13 oz) cans cannellini beans, rinsed and drained

Combine octopus and remaining ingredients in a bowl, cover and refrigerate for 5 hours or overnight.

To make Parsley & White Bean Salad, heat oil in a saucepan and cook onion, covered, over low heat for about 20 minutes or until very soft, adding a little water if onion is sticking to pan. Remove onion from pan and combine with remaining ingredients in a bowl. Season to taste and toss gently.

Cook octopus in batches on a chargrill, or on the flat plate of a barbecue, until just changed in colour. Serve the salad topped with octopus, and with lemon wedges on the side.

SERVES 4

Octopus can be marinated a day ahead.

seafood salad with peas, beans & tarragon dressing

This salad is one of our favourites. It uses a combination of prawns, calamari and mussels but is just as lovely if you use prawns only. You can buy cooked prawns but we like to steam them ourselves because the texture and flavour are more delicate.

12 medium green prawns (shrimp), peeled and deveined, tails intact

2 medium calamari, cleaned, cut into 1 cm ($\frac{1}{2}$ in) thick rings

500 g (1 lb) black mussels, scrubbed and bearded

200 g (6$\frac{1}{2}$ oz) broadbeans (fava beans), podded (about 500 g/1 lb in pods)

100 g (3$\frac{1}{2}$ oz) peas, podded (about 250 g/8 oz in pods)

2 cups baby salad leaves

1 avocado, chopped

TARRAGON DRESSING

1 tbsp chopped fresh tarragon

1 tbsp tarragon vinegar

$\frac{1}{4}$ cup (2 fl oz) extra virgin olive oil

1 vine-ripened tomato, peeled, seeded, finely chopped

To make Tarragon Dressing, combine all ingredients and season to taste.

Cook prawns and calamari in batches in the top of a double steamer over simmering water for about 1 minute or until just cooked. Drain well and transfer to a bowl, then stir in half the dressing.

Place mussels in a large saucepan with 2 tablespoons water and cook, covered, over medium heat until mussels open. Drain mussels and, when cool enough to handle, remove mussel meat and add to prawn mixture.

Cook broadbeans in simmering salted water for 2 minutes. Drain, then rinse under cold water and shell. Cook peas in simmering salted water for 5 minutes. Drain, rinse under cold water.

Toss salad leaves with half remaining dressing and divide among plates. Top with avocado, broadbeans, peas and seafood mixture. Spoon remaining dressing around plate.

SERVES 4

Dressing can be made 2 hours ahead.

GLUTEN-FREE ✓   DAIRY-FREE ✓   DETOX-FRIENDLY ✓

chilli crab with soft polenta

This recipe was inspired by a dish that Kathy had at Bondi's Icebergs restaurant, in Sydney. The combination of textures and flavours is sensational and it's such a simple dish to prepare, especially if you use pre-steamed polenta, which only takes about 5 minutes to cook. Follow the directions on the packet.

extra virgin olive oil

2 small fresh red chillies, seeded, finely
    chopped

2 cloves garlic, finely chopped

1 eschalot (French shallot), finely
    chopped

400 g (13 oz) crab meat

1 tbsp finely chopped fresh dill

sprigs of fresh dill and lemon wedges,
    to serve

SOFT POLENTA

1 litre (32 fl oz) Chicken Stock
    (page 174)

100 g (3 1/2 oz) polenta (yellow
    cornmeal)

ROCKET & ZUCCHINI SALAD

1 green zucchini (courgette)

1 yellow zucchini (courgette)

2 tbsp extra virgin olive oil

2 tsp lemon juice

2 cups rocket (arugula) leaves

1 tbsp toasted pinenuts

To make Soft Polenta, bring stock to the boil and whisk in polenta and season with salt. Cook polenta over lowest heat, stirring regularly with a whisk for about 30 minutes or until soft. The polenta should be soft and flowing – if it is too stiff, add a little more hot stock or boiling water.

To make Rocket & Zucchini Salad, cut zucchini into fine ribbons, using a mandolin if possible. Combine oil and lemon juice, season to taste, then toss gently with zucchini and remaining ingredients.

Heat 2 tablespoons oil in a saucepan and cook chilli, garlic and eschalot over low heat until soft. Remove from heat, stir in crab meat and dill and season to taste.

Spoon soft polenta into shallow bowls, top with crab mixture and sprigs of dill and drizzle with a little more oil. Serve with lemon wedges and Rocket & Zucchini Salad.

SERVES 4

Best made just before serving.

seared tuna with panzanella & caper dressing

Panzanella is a traditional Italian-style bread salad, which goes well with many dishes including beef and lamb. If you don't have time to make your own gluten-free bread, buy a loaf from a health food store. We suggest you cook the tuna on one side only – give it a try.

4 X 100 g (3 1/2 oz) thin tuna fillets
olive oil
fresh baby basil leaves, lemon wedges and
  Leafy Green Salad (page 176), to serve

CAPER DRESSING

2 tsp baby capers
1/4 preserved lemon, skin only,
  finely chopped
1 eschallot (French shallot), finely chopped
1 tbsp lemon juice
2 tbsp extra virgin olive oil

PANZANELLA

2 tomatoes, chopped into 1 cm
  (1/2 in) pieces
3 slices Yeast-free Hi-fibre Bread
  (page 146), crusts removed, chopped into
  1 cm (1/2 in) pieces
1/2 red capsicum (pepper), chopped into
  1 cm (1/2 in) pieces
1/2 yellow capsicum (pepper), chopped into
  1 cm (1/2 in) pieces
1/4 cup (1 1/2 oz) baby black olives
1/4 cup firmly packed torn fresh basil leaves
2 tbsp extra virgin olive oil

To make Caper Dressing, combine all ingredients, season to taste and stand for 1 hour for flavours to develop.

To make Panzanella, combine all ingredients, season to taste and stand for 1 hour for flavours to develop and for bread to soften and soak up the tomato juices.

Brush tuna with oil on one side and cook on that side over high heat in a non-stick frying pan, pressing down with a spatula, until well browned. Do not cook the other side.

Place tuna, seared-side up, on a bed of Panzanella. Drizzle with Caper Dressing, sprinkle with basil leaves and serve with lemon wedges and salad.

SERVES 4

Panzanella and dressing can be prepared 3 hours ahead.

whiting parcels
with roasted fennel salad

Whiting is a delicate fish and has a soft, sweet flavour. It has tiny bones, which you really should try to remove before you make this recipe. The Roasted Fennel Salad is also an excellent accompaniment to a simple fillet of grilled fish.

grated rind of 2 lemons

1 cup chopped mixed fresh herbs
   including flat-leaf (Italian) parsley, dill,
   basil, mint

1/2 red (Spanish) onion, finely chopped

8 x 100 g (3 1/2 oz) whiting fillets,
   skinned

16 anchovies, drained on paper towel

1 quantity Aioli (page 177), to serve
   (optional)

Leafy Green Salad (page 176), to serve

ROASTED FENNEL SALAD

600 g (1 lb 3 oz) bulb fennel, trimmed,
   sliced

extra virgin olive oil

12 spears asparagus, trimmed

2 zucchini (courgette), cut into 6
   lengthwise, halved crosswise

1 orange, peeled, segmented

1 tbsp toasted pinenuts

To make Roasted Fennel Salad, place fennel on an oven tray, toss with a little oil and season to taste. Roast at 200°C (400°F), stirring occasionally, for 20 minutes or until browned. Place asparagus and zucchini on another oven tray, brush with a little oil and roast at 200°C (400°F), turning occasionally, for 10 minutes or until tender. Combine fennel, asparagus, zucchini, orange segments and pinenuts in a bowl and season to taste.

Combine lemon rind, herbs and onion and season to taste.

Lie whiting fillets skinned-side down and top each fillet with 2 anchovy fillets. Spoon the lemon and herb stuffing over the top, then roll fillets around stuffing and place in a baking dish. Cover with foil and bake at 180°C (350°F) for 10–15 minutes or until whiting is just cooked. Remove from oven and stand for 10 minutes before serving.

Place whiting parcels on a plate and drizzle with a little aioli, if using. Serve with Roasted Fennel Salad and green salad.

SERVES 4

Salad can be prepared 2 hours ahead.

GLUTEN-FREE ✔   DAIRY-FREE ✔   DETOX-FRIENDLY ✔

buckwheat pasta with clams

Clams are easy to cook and traditionally go well with pasta. Check with your fishmonger that they have been degorged because they can be full of sand. Just to make sure, soak them in cold water for 2 hours before using. If you are on a detox, omit the white wine and use stock or water.

1 tbsp olive oil

2 eschalots (French shallots), thinly sliced

2 cloves garlic, chopped

2 tomatoes, peeled, seeded, chopped

¼ cup (2 fl oz) dry white wine

good pinch saffron threads

1 kg (2 lb) clams, soaked in cold water
   for 2 hours, drained

250 g (8 oz) buckwheat pasta

1 tbsp shredded fresh basil leaves

1 tbsp coarsely chopped fresh flat-leaf
   (Italian) parsley leaves

Heat oil in a large saucepan and cook eschalots and garlic over low heat until soft. Add tomatoes and cook over high heat until pulpy. Add wine and saffron, bring to the boil and simmer for 1 minute.

Add clams, cover with a tight fitting lid and cook over medium heat, stirring occasionally, until clams open.

Meanwhile, cook pasta in simmering water for about 7 minutes or until al dente. Drain and toss with clam mixture, basil and parsley.

SERVES 4

Best made just before serving.

middle eastern lentils & rice with cabbage salad

This dish was inspired by Lona Jones, who cooks a variation of this recipe for lunch at Manna from Heaven. It's a simple earthy dish that is great comfort food, as well as being truly delicious.

½ cup (3½ oz) green lentils

2 tbsp olive oil

2 onions, halved, sliced

1 cup (6½ oz) long-grain rice

2 cups (16 fl oz) hot Vegetable Stock or Chicken Stock (page 174) or water

¼ cup chopped fresh coriander (cilantro)

¼ cup (1½ oz) toasted pinenuts

CABBAGE SALAD

400 g (13 oz) savoy cabbage, finely shredded

2 cloves garlic, finely chopped

3 vine-ripened tomatoes, chopped

For Cabbage Salad, combine all ingredients and season to taste. Stand for 1 hour for flavours to develop.

Rinse lentils and cook in simmering water for 10 minutes. Drain.

Heat oil in a saucepan and cook onions over low heat until very soft and just beginning to brown, adding a little water if sticking to pan.

Remove half of the onion and reserve. Add rice to remaining onion in pan and stir over medium heat for 1 minute. Add hot stock or water, season to taste and bring to the boil. Stir in lentils, reduce heat to low, then cover and cook for 10 minutes. Turn off heat and stand for 10 minutes, then fluff with a fork and stir in coriander and pinenuts.

Serve lentils and rice topped with reserved onions, and with Cabbage Salad.

SERVES 4

Lentil and rice mixture can be prepared a day ahead.

GLUTEN-FREE ✔ **DAIRY-FREE** ✔ **DETOX-FRIENDLY** ✔ **LUNCH BOX** ✔

sweet corn broth
with chive oil & minced olives

This is a beautifully light soup with a delicate flavour and can be eaten warm or at room temperature. If you want a heartier, chunky soup, use a hand-held blender to blend only half the soup, then leave it unsieved.

½ cup (3½ oz) cannellini beans,
   soaked in cold water overnight

4 corn cobs

olive oil

1 onion, chopped

1 small fresh red chilli, seeded, chopped

2 cloves garlic, chopped

1 large Sebago potato, chopped

6 cups (48 fl oz) Vegetable Stock or
   Chicken Stock (page 174)

¼ cup (1½ oz) black olives, pitted,
   finely chopped

Coriander & Chilli Corn Bread
   (page 145), to serve

CHIVE OIL

¼ cup (2 fl oz) olive oil

2 tbsp chopped fresh chives

For Chive Oil, combine oil and chives and blend with a small hand-held blender. Stand for 1 hour for flavours to develop.

Cook drained cannellini beans in simmering water for about 45 minutes or until soft.

Remove kernels from corn. Heat 1 tablespoon oil in a saucepan and cook onion over low heat until soft. Add corn, cannellini beans, chilli, garlic and potato and stir over medium heat for 1 minute. Add stock, season to taste and bring to the boil, then simmer over low heat for about 30 minutes or until corn and potato are very soft. Cool slightly, transfer soup to a food processor in batches, process until smooth, then sieve.

Reheat soup, check seasoning and serve in warm bowls topped with a drizzle of Chive Oil and a spoonful of minced olives. Serve hot or cold with corn bread.

SERVES 4

Makes 1.8 litres (58 fl oz) half-blended soup or 1.35 litres (43 fl oz) blended and sieved soup

Soup and chive oil can be prepared a day ahead.

vegetable antipasto

By individually plating the antipasto, this becomes a very smart course. If you want a more casual feel, serve each component in bowls for everyone to help themselves. You can substitute the tofu with some chargrilled squid if you are not looking for a vegetarian meal.

extra virgin olive oil

sea salt and freshly ground black pepper

**WHITE BEANS WITH
CHERRY TOMATOES & OLIVES**

1/2 cup (3 1/2 oz) dried white beans,
   soaked in cold water overnight

2 tbsp olive oil

1 large fresh red chilli, sliced

200 g (6 1/2 oz) cherry tomatoes, halved

2 cloves garlic, chopped

6 fresh basil leaves, torn

2 tbsp baby black olives, pitted

**ROASTED CARROTS WITH BALSAMIC
VINEGAR**

4 large carrots

1 tbsp extra virgin olive oil

2 tsp aged balsamic vinegar

2 tsp brown sugar

To make White Beans with Cherry Tomatoes & Olives, cook drained beans in simmering water for about 40 minutes or until beans are tender, then drain. Heat oil in a frying pan, add chilli and tomatoes and cook over high heat for 1 minute. Add beans and garlic, cook for another minute, then season to taste. Cool slightly, then stir in basil and olives.

To make Roasted Carrots with Balsamic Vinegar, shave carrots thinly on a mandolin, place in a bowl and toss with oil, vinegar and sugar and season to taste. Place on an oven tray and roast at 200°C (400°F) for 30–40 minutes, stirring occasionally, until carrots are tender and lightly browned.

GLUTEN-FREE ✔ **DAIRY-FREE** ✔ **DETOX-FRIENDLY** ✔ **LUNCH BOX** ✔

SHAVED FENNEL WITH MUSHROOMS & HAZELNUTS

1 X 500 (1 lb) bulb fennel, trimmed

6 baby Portobello button mushrooms

1 tbsp chopped fresh dill

1/3 cup (1¾ oz) toasted peeled
   hazelnuts, coarsely chopped

2 tsp lemon juice

1 tbsp macadamia oil

GRILLED EGGPLANT & TOFU

450 g (15 oz) eggplant (aubergine),
   sliced 1 cm (½ in) thick

200 g (6½ oz) firm tofu, sliced 1 cm
   (½ in) thick

olive oil

2 tbsp finely chopped fresh flat-leaf
   (Italian) parsley

2 cloves garlic, finely chopped

1 tbsp red wine vinegar

To make Shaved Fennel with Mushrooms & Hazelnuts, shave fennel thinly on a mandolin. Slice mushrooms very thinly. Combine dill, hazelnuts, lemon juice and oil and season to taste, then toss gently with fennel and mushrooms.

To make Grilled Eggplant & Tofu, brush eggplant and tofu slices with a little oil and grill (broil) or chargrill on both sides until browned. Cut eggplant slices into quarters. Combine parsley, garlic, vinegar and 2 tablespoons oil, season to taste and toss with eggplant. Place tofu on plates and top with eggplant mixture.

Place a serving of each antipasto on plates, then drizzle each plate with a little oil and sprinkle with sea salt and fresh ground black pepper.

SERVES 4 (main course)
SERVES 6 (entree)

Can be prepared a day ahead.

grilled polenta with mushroom ragout & roasted zucchini flowers

We have used a mixture of mushrooms for this recipe. Substitute other varieties if you like. Zucchini flowers are a delight and start to appear in fruit shops in summer. Kathy loves them deep-fried in tempura batter, however, this is an excellent gluten-free alternative.

5½ cups (44 fl oz) Vegetable Stock (page 174) or water

300 g (10 oz) polenta (yellow cornmeal)

100 g (3½ oz) soft tofu

1 clove garlic, chopped

1 tbsp chopped basil

8 small zucchini (courgette) flowers, with baby zucchini attached

olive oil

MUSHROOM RAGOUT

2 tbsp olive oil

1 small onion, chopped

150 g (5 oz) button mushrooms

200 g (6½ oz) large Portobello mushrooms, quartered

150 g (5 oz) oyster mushrooms

2 cloves garlic, chopped

2 tbsp torn fresh basil leaves

⅓ cup (2½ fl oz) Vegetable Stock (page 174) or water

Bring stock or water to the boil in a saucepan, add salt to taste, then reduce heat and whisk in polenta in a thin stream. Reduce heat to very low and cook for about 20 minutes, stirring occasionally with a whisk until all the lumps are gone and mixture comes away from side of pan. Remove from heat. Line a tray with baking paper, spoon polenta onto tray and cool. When cold, cut into 12 fingers and place on an oven tray.

Combine tofu, garlic and basil in the small bowl of a food processor, season to taste and process until smooth.

Gently prise open zucchini flowers and, using a teaspoon, fill centre with tofu mixture. Brush flowers and zucchini with oil and roast at 200°C (400°F) for 10 minutes or until flower is crisp and zucchini is tender.

Brush polenta with oil and grill (broil) on both sides until golden.

To make Mushroom Ragout, heat oil in a wok and cook onion over high heat until golden. Add mushrooms and stir-fry over high heat until wilted. Add garlic and stir-fry for a few seconds, then add basil and stock or water and cook over high heat for another 2 minutes.

Spoon Mushroom Ragout onto grilled polenta and top with roasted zucchini flowers.

SERVES 4

Polenta can be prepared a day ahead.

herbed falafels with hummus & quinoa tabbouleh

Be generous with the salt when seasoning falafels, otherwise they can be quite bland. As a variation, you can add the falafels to our Baby Spinach & Pomegranate Seed Salad (page 176) and serve with toasted Yeast-Free Hi-Fibre Bread (page 146) topped with Roasted Garlic Puree (page 176) or Hummus (page 177).

1 cup (6¼ oz) quinoa

2 cups (16 fl oz) Vegetable Stock (page 174)

6 green (spring) onions (scallions), chopped

1 ½ cups chopped fresh flat-leaf (Italian) parsley

2 tomatoes, finely chopped

¼ cup (2 fl oz) lemon juice

extra virgin olive oil

2 cups (16 ml oz) Hummus (page 177)

HERBED FALAFELS

1 cup (6½ oz) dried broadbeans (fava beans), soaked in cold water overnight

½ cup (3½ oz) dried chickpeas, soaked in cold water overnight

½ cup chopped fresh flat-leaf (Italian) parsley

½ cup chopped fresh coriander (cilantro)

2 tsp ground cumin

2 tsp ground coriander (cilantro)

1 tsp bicarbonate of soda (baking soda)

6 green (spring) onions (scallions) chopped

2 cloves garlic, chopped

1 heaped tsp sea salt

freshly ground black pepper

olive oil

To make Herbed Falafels, combine drained uncooked broadbeans and chickpeas in a food processor and process until they resemble breadcrumbs. Add herbs, spices, bicarbonate of soda, green onions and garlic and season to taste with sea salt and black pepper. Add 3–4 tablespoons water and process until well combined and mixture forms a coarse paste. Cover and refrigerate for 30 minutes.

Using wet hands, shape heaped tablespoons of falafel mixture into small flat patties, pressing mixture together firmly. Place falafels on a greased oven tray, brush lightly with oil and roast at 200°C (400°F) for 10 minutes, then turn and roast for another 5 minutes.

Combine quinoa and stock in a saucepan and bring to the boil, then simmer, covered, over medium heat for 15 minutes or until most of the stock has absorbed and quinoa is tender. Remove lid and stir over heat until any remaining stock has evaporated. Cool. Stir in green onions, parsley, tomatoes, lemon juice and 1 tablespoon oil and season to taste.

Serve Quinoa Tabbouleh topped with Herbed Falafels and Hummus. Drizzle with extra virgin olive oil.

MAKES ABOUT 20 FALAFELS

Tabbouleh can be prepared a day ahead.

GLUTEN-FREE ✓   DAIRY-FREE ✓   DETOX-FRIENDLY ✓   LUNCH BOX ✓

two ways with asparagus

You have two dishes here and it's fun to serve them together, with the soup in little cups on the side. Served this way, the recipe makes enough for four people. However, if you like the idea of the soup on its own, serve it with Yeast-free Hi-fibre Bread (page 146), topped with Hummus (page 177), but there will only be enough for two.

20 spears asparagus, trimmed

olive oil

400 g (13 oz) firm tofu, drained, sliced 1 cm (½ in) thick

4 tomatoes, peeled, chopped

2 cloves garlic, finely chopped

1 tsp fresh thyme leaves

ASPARAGUS SOUP

1 tbsp olive oil

1 onion, chopped

1 clove garlic, chopped

300 g (10 oz) trimmed, chopped asparagus

1 large potato, chopped

600 ml (19 fl oz) Vegetable Stock (page 174) or water, approximately

1 tbsp lemon juice

2 tsp fresh thyme leaves, to serve

extra virgin olive oil, to serve

To make Asparagus Soup, heat oil in a saucepan and cook onion over low heat until soft. Add garlic, asparagus and potato and stir over medium heat for 1 minute. Add stock or water, season to taste and bring to the boil, then simmer over low heat until vegetables are soft. Using a food processor or hand-held blender, blend soup until smooth, adding a little more hot stock or water if too thick. Check seasoning, then return soup to pan to heat through. Just before serving, stir in lemon juice.

Place asparagus spears on an oven tray, brush with oil and season to taste, then roast at 200°C (400°F) for 12 minutes or until lightly browned.

Heat 1 tablespoon oil in a non-stick frying pan and cook tofu in batches on both sides until browned and hot. Remove from pan, add tomatoes and garlic and cook over high heat until tomatoes are thick and pulpy, then season to taste and stir in thyme.

Serve tofu, topped with asparagus and tomato sauce on a plate, with a little cup of asparagus soup garnished with thyme leaves and a drizzle of extra virgin olive oil on the side.

SERVES 4

Makes about 3 cups (24 fl oz) soup

Soup can be prepared a day ahead, but will lose its vibrant colour.

GLUTEN-FREE ✔   DAIRY-FREE ✔   DETOX-FRIENDLY ✔

warm pumpkin, beetroot & chickpea salad with tahini sauce

We love roasted beetroot. Roasting really brings out the flavour and retains all the goodness. If you can't get baby beetroot use large ones, but you will need to roast them for longer. Don't salt the water when cooking the chickpeas (or any beans and pulses), as it will only make them tough.

1 cup (6½ oz) dried chickpeas, soaked in cold water overnight, drained

½ small red (Spanish) onion, finely chopped

2 tbsp red wine vinegar

extra virgin olive oil

600 g (1 lb 3 oz) butternut pumpkin (squash), peeled, cut into 2 cm (¾ in) pieces

6 baby beetroot (beets), trimmed

2 cups firmly packed watercress or rocket (arugula) leaves

TAHINI SAUCE

¼ cup (2 fl oz) tahini

2 cloves garlic, crushed

2 tbsp lemon juice

1 tbsp extra virgin olive oil

1 tbsp chopped fresh flat-leaf (Italian) parsley

1 tbsp chopped basil

To make Tahini Sauce, combine all ingredients, whisk in ¼ cup (2 fl oz) water and season to taste.

Cook chickpeas in simmering water for about 45 minutes or until tender. Drain. Combine chickpeas, onion, vinegar and ¼ cup (2 fl oz) oil and season to taste.

Meanwhile, place pumpkin on an oven tray and brush with a little oil. Wrap each beetroot in foil and place beside pumpkin. Roast at 200°C (400°F) for 30–45 minutes, turning pumpkin regularly, until pumpkin is browned and beetroot are tender.

When beetroot are cool enough to handle, rub off skins and cut into pieces the same size as the pumpkin.

Place watercress or rocket leaves in shallow bowls and top with chickpea mixture and pumpkin and beetroot, then drizzle with Tahini Sauce.

SERVES 4

Tahini sauce can be prepared a day ahead.

GLUTEN-FREE ✓ DAIRY-FREE ✓ DETOX-FRIENDLY ✓ LUNCH BOX ✓

dinner

KATHY: *At the end of a busy day, what I love to do most is to cook. It helps me to relax and my husband, Peter, and I get to savour the results. I shop for ingredients on my way home from work. If I'm not detoxing, we have a few glasses of wine with dinner: we particularly love pinot noir, as it seems to go with so many food groups. Unless we are entertaining, we only have one course, which always includes lots of vegetables, and we always have a salad. I love seafood and usually order that if we go out for dinner.*

JAN: *Gavin and I always have the 'what's for dinner' conversation either the night before, in the morning or by email during the day. Together we plan what we're having (I am very lucky because he loves cooking just as much as I do) and one of us picks up what we need to make that night's 'creation'. If we are too tired to cook, we always go for good quality Asian takeaway, like Japanese, Vietnamese or Chinese, because it is the far healthier fast food option. As for wine, Gavin keeps a wonderful cellar, so sometimes it can be difficult to stick to my four AFDs (alcohol-free days) a week when we are not detoxing! We always have fruit for dessert and in summer it is often in the form of our Mango Sorbet with Summer Fruit Salsa (page 131).*

Many people tell us how difficult it is to prepare healthy meals during the week, especially if there are children to cook for. We hope our dinner recipes will inspire you to keep your pantry stocked with the essentials, so you need only to pick up a few extras to make terrific meals all through the week.

These recipes have been chosen with the home cook in mind. They are all achievable and suitable for both family eating and entertaining. Some require a little more preparation than others, such as marinating, but on the whole they are quite straightforward.

Stock your pantry with dried goods such as rice, rice noodles, quinoa, polenta, legumes, ground spices and condiments, but make sure they are well within their use-by date or your dish may not taste as good. Like lunch, it's a good idea to plan your dinners around seasonal produce (see our winter and summer menu ideas on pages 172–3).

If you are eating dinner out and have allergies, phone ahead to the restaurant to see if there is anything on the menu that will suit you, or ask the chef to prepare something for you. We have found that, given a little warning, most restaurants are only too happy to oblige.

braised chicken
with middle eastern mash

Kathy likes to use chicken breasts with the skin on for this recipe, for a little added flavour, but to keep Jan happy we have taken it off, to keep the fat content lower – it's up to you. Za'atar is a Middle Eastern spice mix containing sesame seeds, thyme and sumac.

4 skinless chicken breast fillets

olive oil

1 tbsp za'atar

1/3 cup (2 1/2 fl oz) dry white wine

1/3 cup (2 1/2 fl oz) Chicken Stock
   (page 174)

1/4 cup (1 1/2 oz) toasted pinenuts

1/4 cup (1 1/4 oz) currants

Rocket & Pear Salad (page 175),
   to serve

MIDDLE EASTERN MASH

1/2 tsp cumin seeds

600 g (1 lb 3 oz) Sebago potatoes

600 ml (19 fl oz) Chicken Stock
   (page 174), approximately

1 tbsp olive oil

1 small onion, chopped

2 cloves garlic, chopped

2 tbsp chopped fresh coriander
   (cilantro)

To make Middle Eastern Mash, dry-fry cumin seeds in a non-stick frying pan until aromatic. Coarsely grind with a mortar and pestle.

Cover potatoes with stock and bring to the boil, then simmer, uncovered, over low heat until tender. Drain and reserve stock.

Heat oil in a saucepan and cook onion over low heat until soft and just beginning to brown. Add ground cumin and garlic to pan and cook over low heat until aromatic. Mash potatoes with enough stock to form a smooth mash, then stir in onion mixture and coriander and season to taste.

Meanwhile, rub chicken breasts with a little oil and za'atar and season to taste. Heat 1 tablespoon oil in a non-stick frying pan and cook chicken in batches over high heat until browned. Remove from pan and place in a casserole dish. Deglaze pan with wine and stock and bring to the boil. Add pan juices to casserole dish, cover and bake at 180°C (350°F) for 10 minutes, then add pinenuts and currants and bake for another 5–10 minutes, depending on thickness, or until chicken is cooked through. Remove chicken from pan and check seasoning for sauce.

Place mash on a plate, top with sliced chicken and drizzle over pan juices, currants and pinenuts. Serve with Rocket & Pear Salad.

SERVES 4

Best made just before serving.

GLUTEN-FREE ✔   **DAIRY-FREE** ✔   **DETOX-FRIENDLY** ✔

portuguese-style duck rice

Duck is a very fatty bird, and this is a great way to prepare it – it still retains all the flavour but doesn't have the fat. This splendidly rustic dish can also be made with poached chicken.

olive oil

2 onions, chopped

2 cloves garlic, chopped

1 bay leaf

100 g (3 1/2 oz) prosciutto, trimmed of
   fat, chopped

1 1/2 cups (10 oz) long-grain rice

1 egg yolk, beaten with 1 tbsp cold water

150 g (5 oz) fresh breadcrumbs made
   from gluten-free bread

600 g (1 lb 3 oz) baby green beans,
   trimmed

2 cloves garlic, extra, chopped

POACHED DUCK

2 kg (4 lb) duck

2 black peppercorns

2 tsp salt

2 onions, halved

2 cloves garlic

1 bay leaf

SERVES 4–6

Duck can be poached a day ahead.

To make Poached Duck, wash duck, place in a large saucepan and cover with water. Add remaining ingredients and bring slowly to the boil, skimming any scum that rises to the surface. Cook duck over low heat for about 1 hour or until juices run clear when the thigh is pierced with a knife. Remove duck, strain stock and, when cool, skim fat from surface. When duck is cool enough to handle, remove skin and bones and cut meat into bite-sized pieces.

Heat 1 tablespoon oil in a saucepan, add onions, garlic and bay leaf and cook over low heat until onions are soft, adding a little stock if onions are sticking to pan. Add prosciutto and stir over medium heat until golden. Stir in duck meat and season to taste.

Heat 2 1/4 cups (18 fl oz) reserved duck stock in a saucepan, add rice and simmer, covered, over low heat for 10 minutes or until rice is just cooked and stock is absorbed. Stand, covered, for 10 minutes, then season to taste and fluff with a fork.

Spoon three-quarters of the rice mixture into an 8-cup (64 fl oz) capacity ovenproof dish and top with duck mixture. Spoon remaining rice over, brush with egg yolk mixture and sprinkle with breadcrumbs. Bake at 170°C (325°F) for 30 minutes or until breadcrumbs are golden and rice is hot.

Meanwhile, cook beans in simmering salted water for about 5 minutes, until just tender, then drain and rinse under cold water. Heat 1 tablespoon oil in a saucepan and cook extra garlic for 30 seconds, then add beans, toss to combine and season to taste. Serve duck rice with garlic beans.

marinated chicken with saffron onions & quinoa

Quinoa is a great substitute for couscous or burghul (cracked wheat). It can be quite bland, but is an excellent carrier of flavours, particularly those of the Mediterranean. Kathy tested this recipe with a bunch of friends and they all loved it, especially the sweet saffron-flavoured onions.

extra virgin olive oil

1/2 tsp each ground ginger, cumin, sweet paprika and cinnamon

6 skinless chicken thigh fillets

2 tbsp lemon juice

pinch saffron threads, to taste

2 onions, halved, sliced

1/4 cup firmly packed fresh flat-leaf (Italian) parsley leaves

QUINOA

2 cups (16 fl oz) Chicken Stock (page 174)

2 cloves garlic, chopped

1 cup (6 1/4 oz) quinoa

1/3 cup (1 3/4 oz) green olives, pitted and sliced

1/4 preserved lemon, skin only, chopped

1 tbsp chopped fresh flat-leaf (Italian) parsley

1 tbsp chopped fresh coriander (cilantro)

Combine 1 tablespoon oil and spices and rub into chicken with lemon juice. Cover and marinate in refrigerator for 5 hours or overnight.

Heat 1 tablespoon oil in a non-stick frying pan and cook chicken in batches until browned. Transfer to an oven tray and roast at 200°C (400°F) for 15–20 minutes or until cooked. Rest in a warm place, loosely covered, for 10 minutes before cutting each thigh fillet into 3 pieces.

Meanwhile, cover saffron with 1 tablespoon boiling water and stand for 5 minutes. Heat 1 tablespoon oil in a saucepan, add onions and saffron mixture and cook, covered, over low heat for about 20 minutes or until very soft, adding a little water if sticking to pan. Remove lid and stir over high heat until onions are golden, then season to taste.

To make Quinoa, bring stock slowly to the boil. Add garlic and quinoa and cook, covered, over low heat for 15 minutes or until stock is absorbed and quinoa is tender. Stir in olives, preserved lemon and herbs and season to taste.

Serve chicken on a bed of quinoa, topped with saffron onions and sprinkled with parsley.

SERVES 4

Quinoa can be prepared a day ahead.

GLUTEN-FREE ✔ **DAIRY-FREE** ✔ **DETOX-FRIENDLY** ✔ **LUNCH BOX** ✔

greek-style roast chicken with avgolemono sauce

There are so many ways to roast a chicken, and this is just one of them. It's Kathy's favourite dish and she cooks it most Sunday evenings, varying the flavours. The key element is to buy the best free-range or organic chicken and to keep the recipe simple. Jan recommends that if you're trying to reduce your cholesterol, don't eat the skin and only have a drizzle of the sauce.

1 cup (6 1/2 oz) long-grain rice

olive oil

1 leek, trimmed, chopped

2 tbsp toasted pinenuts

1 tbsp chopped fresh dill

grated rind of 1 lemon

1.8 kg (3 lb10 oz) free-range chicken

1 tbsp dried oregano

2 bunches English spinach, wilted,
   to serve

AVGOLEMONO SAUCE

3 egg yolks

1/2 cup (4 fl oz) strained lemon juice

1 cup (8 fl oz) hot Chicken Stock
   (page 174)

Cook rice in simmering salted water for 10 minutes. Drain and rinse under cold water. Heat 1 tablespoon oil in a saucepan and cook leek, covered, over low heat until soft. Combine rice, leek, pinenuts, dill and lemon rind and season to taste.

Rinse chicken and pat dry with paper towel. Spoon enough rice mixture into chicken to fill cavity and tie legs together with string. Reserve remaining rice mixture to serve with chicken.

Place chicken in a roasting pan, brush with oil, season to taste and sprinkle with oregano. Pour 1 cup (8 fl oz) water around chicken and roast at 200°C (400°F) for 1 1/4 hours or until juices run clear. Remove from pan and rest, loosely covered, in a warm place for 15 minutes. Strain pan juices, skim off any fat and add juices to reserved rice mixture in a saucepan. Reheat gently.

To make Avgolemono Sauce, whisk egg yolks for about 2 minutes or until pale and frothy. Add lemon juice and a third of the hot stock, whisking continuously. Whisk in remaining stock, then transfer mixture to a small saucepan. Cook sauce over very low heat, without boiling, for about 4 minutes, stirring continuously with a wooden spoon, until sauce coats the back of the spoon, then season to taste.

Serve chicken on a bed of wilted spinach drizzled with Avgolemono Sauce. Spoon rice stuffing and reserved rice mixture on one side.

SERVES 4

Best made just before serving.

GLUTEN-FREE ✔ DAIRY-FREE ✔ DETOX-FRIENDLY ✔ LUNCH BOX ✔

sesame chicken
with rice noodles & cashews

This simple stir-fry is an ideal dish to cook when you are short on time. Serve it on a large platter and place in the centre of the table, for family and friends to help themselves. Use thinly sliced fillet of beef or pork instead of the chicken.

500 g (1 lb) chicken thigh fillets, trimmed of fat and thinly sliced

¼ cup (2 fl oz) wheat-free tamari sauce

1 tbsp mirin

1 tbsp finely chopped fresh ginger

vegetable oil

1 tsp sesame oil

1 red (Spanish) onion, halved and thinly sliced

2 cloves garlic, chopped

1 tsp brown sugar

juice and grated rind of 1 lemon

2 bunches asparagus, trimmed and halved crosswise

120 g (4 oz) sugar snap peas, trimmed

1 tbsp toasted sesame seeds

150 g (5 oz) rice noodles, cooked according to directions on packet

2 tbsp chopped toasted cashews

2 green (spring) onions (scallions), thinly sliced

Combine chicken, 1 tablespoon tamari, mirin and ginger in a bowl, then cover and refrigerate for 2 hours.

Heat 1 tablespoon vegetable oil and the sesame oil in a wok and cook chicken mixture in batches over high heat, then remove from wok. Add a little more vegetable oil, if necessary, and cook onion over medium heat until golden, then remove from wok. Add remaining tamari, the garlic, sugar, lemon juice and rind to wok and stir over heat until combined. Add asparagus and sugar snap peas and stir-fry for 1 minute. Return chicken and onion to pan, add sesame seeds and stir to combine.

Spoon rice noodles into shallow bowls, top with chicken mixture and sprinkle with cashews and green onions.

SERVES 4

Best made just before serving.

citrus spatchcocks with warm chickpeas & almonds

This recipe was inspired by a dish Kathy had at the Botanical Gardens restaurant in Adelaide – the combination of poultry and citrus works well. To save time, or if you forget to soak the chickpeas, use rinsed and drained canned ones.

4 spatchcocks (poussin)

100 g (3 1/2 oz) chickpeas, soaked in cold water overnight, drained

olive oil

80 g (2 1/2 oz) toasted whole raw or blanched almonds

fresh sprigs of thyme and Leafy Green Salad (page 177), to serve

MARINADE

1 tbsp fresh thyme leaves

1 tbsp dried oregano

4 strips lemon rind

1/4 cup (2 fl oz) lemon juice

4 strips orange rind

1/4 cup (2 fl oz) orange juice

1 tbsp balsamic vinegar

2 tbsp olive oil

4 cloves garlic, halved

AVOCADO SALSA

1 avocado, chopped

1/2 small red (Spanish) onion, chopped

1 tbsp chopped fresh oregano

1 tbsp lemon juice

1 tbsp extra virgin olive oil

To make Marinade, combine all ingredients and season to taste. Place spatchcocks in a large dish, pour marinade over, then cover and refrigerate for 5 hours or overnight.

Cook chickpeas in simmering water for about 45 minutes or until tender, then drain.

Drain spatchcocks and reserve marinade. Place spatchcocks, breast-side up, in a roasting pan, pour marinade over and add 1/2 cup (4 fl oz) water. Brush spatchcocks with a little oil and season to taste. Roast at 200°C (400°F) for 40 minutes, brushing with the marinade from time to time, or until cooked. Remove spatchcocks and rest, loosely covered, in a warm place for 10 minutes.

Drain pan juices, skim fat and place in a saucepan with chickpeas and almonds. Bring to the boil, then simmer over low heat for 5 minutes. Season to taste.

To make Avocado Salsa, combine all ingredients and season to taste.

Spoon chickpea mixture onto plates and top with spatchcocks and sprigs of thyme. Place the salsa to one side and serve with the green salad.

SERVES 4

Spatchcocks can be marinated a day ahead.

GLUTEN-FREE ✓ DAIRY-FREE ✓ DETOX-FRIENDLY ✓ LUNCH BOX ✓

chicken laksa with rice noodles

Look for a prepared laksa paste in your local supermarket or food store. Check the list of ingredients to make sure it is gluten-free. You can add sliced tofu instead of chicken if you want a vegetarian dish.

vegetable oil

2 eschalots (French shallots), thinly sliced

1 onion, halved, sliced

1/2 red capsicum (pepper), thinly sliced

1/2 cup (4 fl oz) prepared vegetarian laksa paste

4 cups (32 fl oz) Vegetable Stock (page 174) or water

1 cup (8 fl oz) light coconut milk

400 g (13 oz) skinless chicken breast fillets, thinly sliced

100 g (3 1/2 oz) snowpeas (mangetout), trimmed, halved lengthwise

200 g (6 1/2 oz) thick dried rice (stick) noodles

125 g (4 oz) bean sprouts, trimmed

1 Lebanese (small green) cucumber, halved, seeds removed, sliced

50 g (1 3/4 oz) snowpea sprouts

fresh coriander (cilantro) and mint leaves and lime wedges, to serve

Heat 2 tablespoons oil in a small saucepan and cook eschalots over medium heat until crisp and golden. Drain on paper towel.

Heat 1 tablespoon oil in a large saucepan and cook onion and capsicum over low heat until soft. Add laksa paste and stir over medium heat for 3 minutes. Stir in combined stock or water and coconut milk and simmer over medium heat for 5 minutes. Add chicken and snowpeas and simmer gently for another 2 minutes, then add salt to taste.

Meanwhile, cook noodles in simmering water for 5–8 minutes or until tender, drain and place in serving bowls. Top noodles with chicken mixture, bean sprouts, cucumber, snowpea sprouts and herbs, then sprinkle with crisp eschalots. Serve with lime wedges.

SERVES 4

Best made just before serving.

GLUTEN FREE ✔ **DAIRY FREE** ✔ **DETOX FRIENDLY** ✔ **LUNCHBOX** ✔

roasted quail with chargrilled pineapple & warm potato salad

Quail and pineapple might seem like an unusual mix, however, the flavours work really well together. We came across this combination when figs were out of season and we were looking for something with a little sweetness to go with the dish. You can also make this recipe with duck breasts.

4 large quail

2 tsp fresh thyme leaves

balsamic vinegar

extra virgin olive oil

400 g (13 oz) peas, podded
  (about 1 kg/2 lb in pods)

2 thick slices pineapple, quartered

baby salad leaves, to serve

WARM POTATO SALAD

600 g (1 lb 3 oz) kipfler or other waxy
  salad potatoes

1 red (Spanish) onion, halved, sliced

2 tbsp capers

2 tbsp cornichons, sliced

1/3 cup firmly packed fresh flat-leaf
  (Italian) parsley leaves

2 tbsp extra virgin olive oil

1 tbsp white wine vinegar

Combine quail, thyme, 1 tablespoon balsamic vinegar and 1 tablespoon extra virgin olive oil, season to taste, then cover and marinate for 2 hours.

To make Warm Potato Salad, cook potatoes in simmering salted water until tender. Drain and when cool enough to handle, peel and slice thickly. Combine onion and remaining ingredients and season to taste. Toss warm potatoes with onion mixture.

Heat a little oil in a non-stick frying pan and cook drained quail over high heat until browned all over. Place quail on an oven tray and roast at 200°C (400°F) for 10 minutes. Rest, loosely covered, in a warm place for 5 minutes.

Meanwhile, cook peas in simmering salted water until tender. Drain and return to pan, season to taste then crush gently with a potato masher.

Brush pineapple with oil and chargrill until browned on both sides.

Spoon crushed peas onto plates, top with salad leaves and roasted quail, and place pineapple to one side. Drizzle with a little balsamic vinegar and extra virgin olive oil and serve with Warm Potato Salad.

SERVES 4

Potato salad can be prepared a day ahead and reheated to serve.

chicken, green lentil & sweet potato curry

This is a very versatile curry, quick to make and high on flavour. If you want to make this a vegetarian course, leave out the chicken and add more vegetables or tofu. The secret to making a good curry is to check that your spices are fresh (check the use-by date) and to cook them until they are aromatic and have lost their 'raw' taste.

vegetable oil

1 onion, chopped

4 cloves garlic, chopped

4 cm (1 1/2 in) piece fresh ginger, peeled, chopped

1 cup (6 1/2 oz) green lentils

300 g (10 oz) orange sweet potato, chopped

1 potato, chopped

500 g (1 lb) chicken thigh fillets, halved

1/2 tsp ground turmeric

1 tsp ground cumin

1 tsp ground coriander

1 tsp garam masala

1/2 tsp ground chilli, or to taste

2 tomatoes, chopped

3 large fresh green chillies, seeded, chopped

1 tsp brown sugar

juice of 1 lime

2 tbsp chopped fresh dill

1/4 cup fresh mint leaves

1/4 cup fresh coriander (cilantro) leaves

Steamed Ginger Rice (page 178), to serve

Heat 1 tablespoon oil in a large saucepan and cook onion, garlic and ginger over low heat until soft. Add lentils, sweet potato and potato and 3 cups (24 fl oz) water and simmer over low heat for 20 minutes or until lentils and potatoes are almost soft.

Meanwhile, heat 1 tablespoon oil in a frying pan and cook chicken in batches over medium heat until browned. Remove from pan, then add turmeric, cumin, ground coriander, garam masala and ground chilli and stir over heat until aromatic, adding a little more oil if necessary. Add tomatoes, green chillies and 1/2 cup (4 fl oz) water and cook until tomatoes are thick and pulpy. Stir into lentil mixture, add chicken and sugar, then cover and cook over low heat for about 10 minutes or until chicken is cooked.

Stir in lime juice and herbs and season with salt. Serve with Steamed Ginger Rice.

SERVES 4–6

Curry can be prepared a day ahead.

GLUTEN-FREE ✔ **DAIRY-FREE** ✔ **DETOX-FRIENDLY** ✔ **LUNCH BOX** ✔

lamb cutlets with chickpea puree & warm cauliflower salad

You can use canned chickpeas in this recipe if you are in a hurry, although they will give you a slightly different texture. You will need 2–3 cups of canned chickpeas, drained well and rinsed under lots of cold water. The cauliflower salad also goes well with a grilled steak.

olive oil

1 leek, trimmed and cut into
 1 cm (1/2 in) rings

1/4 cup (1 1/2 oz) pinenuts

1/4 cup (1 1/2 oz) sultanas

1 tbsp chopped fresh flat-leaf
 (Italian) parsley

750 g (1 1/2 lb) cauliflower,
 trimmed and broken into florets

1 bay leaf

12 lamb cutlets

lemon wedges, to serve

CHICKPEA PUREE

1 cup (6 1/2 oz) dried chickpeas, soaked
 in cold water overnight, drained

2 tbsp lemon juice

1/2 tsp cumin seeds

1/2 tsp coriander seeds

1 tbsp olive oil

1 small onion, chopped

2 cloves garlic, chopped

1 tbsp chopped fresh flat-leaf (Italian) parsley

1 tbsp chopped fresh coriander (cilantro)

To make Chickpea Puree, cook drained chickpeas in simmering water for 45 minutes or until soft. Drain and reserve cooking liquid. Puree two-thirds of the chickpeas in a food processor, adding lemon juice and enough reserved cooking liquid to form a smooth puree. Stir in remaining whole chickpeas.

Dry-fry cumin and coriander seeds in a non-stick frying pan until aromatic. Coarsely grind in a mortar and pestle.

Heat oil in a frying pan and cook onion over low heat until soft. Add garlic and ground seeds and cook until aromatic. Add chickpea mixture and herbs, then stir until well combined and heated through.

Heat 1 tablespoon oil in a frying pan and cook leek over low heat, stirring occasionally, until soft. Add pinenuts and sultanas and stir until pinenuts are golden. Stir in parsley and season to taste.

Cook cauliflower in simmering salted water with the bay leaf for about 5 minutes or until just tender. Drain and toss gently with leek mixture and 1 tablespoon of oil.

Brush lamb cutlets with a little oil and grill (broil) or barbecue on a flat plate, on both sides until just cooked.

Spoon Chickpea Puree onto plates and top with lamb cutlets. Serve cauliflower mixture and lemon wedges to one side.

SERVES 4

Chickpea puree can be prepared a day ahead.

GLUTEN-FREE ✔ **DAIRY-FREE** ✔ **DETOX-FRIENDLY** ✔ **LUNCH BOX** ✔

lamb backstraps with mushroom risotto & parsley puree

We have chosen lamb backstraps for this recipe because they are very lean. You could use grilled lamb cutlets or roasted and sliced lamb rump. The risotto is also delicious on its own, with the addition of some toasted pinenuts, or you could serve it with roast chicken.

½ cup firmly packed fresh flat-leaf
  (Italian) parsley leaves

2 cloves garlic, chopped

2 tbsp verjuice

1 tsp gluten-free tarragon mustard

olive oil

750 g (1 ½ lb) lamb backstraps
  (eye of loin)

Baby Spinach & Pomegranate Seed
  Salad (page 176), to serve

MUSHROOM RISOTTO

10 g (⅓ oz) dried porcini mushrooms

4 cups (32 fl oz) Chicken Stock
  (page 174), approximately

olive oil

250 g (8 oz) small Portobello
  mushrooms, chopped

1 leek, white part only, chopped

2 cloves garlic, chopped

1 cup (6½ oz) arborio rice

SERVES 4

Best made just before serving.

To make Mushroom Risotto, cover dried mushrooms with ¼ cup (2 fl oz) boiling water and stand for 15 minutes. Drain, reserve liquid then add liquid to chicken stock. Chop mushrooms finely.

Heat 2 teaspoons oil in a deep wide frying pan, add fresh mushrooms and ¼ cup (2 fl oz) stock mixture and cook over high heat until mushrooms are soft. Remove from pan and set aside.

Heat 1 tablespoon oil in a large saucepan and cook leek, covered, over low heat until soft. Add chopped dried mushrooms, garlic and rice and stir over medium heat for 1 minute until rice is coated. Have remaining stock mixture simmering in another saucepan. Add 1 cup (8 fl oz) stock to the rice and stir over heat until stock is absorbed. Add remaining stock ½ cup (4 fl oz) at a time, stirring constantly, allowing each addition to be absorbed before adding the next. With the last addition of stock, add sautéed fresh mushrooms. Remove from heat, cover and stand for 5 minutes.

Meanwhile, place parsley, garlic, verjuice and mustard in a food processor and process until well combined. Add 2 tablespoons oil, season to taste and process until smooth.

Brush lamb with a little oil and seal in a hot non-stick frying pan until brown all over. Transfer to an oven tray and roast at 200°C (400°F) for 7 minutes for pink lamb. Remove from oven and rest, loosely covered, in a warm place for 5 minutes.

Serve risotto in individual bowls, topped with sliced lamb and some parsley puree, with a big bowl of the salad to share.

poached beef with salsa verde

This is a special occasion dish, when you want to treat yourself or if you are entertaining. It's wonderfully light for a meat dish, but still full of flavour. This recipe was inspired by a dish Kathy had at Franklin Manor in Strahan, Tasmania.

4 x 180 g (6 oz) pieces fillet of beef

4 Sebago potatoes, peeled, quartered

2 tsp gluten-free seeded mustard

12 spears asparagus, trimmed and
   steamed, to serve

POACHING STOCK

6 cups (48 fl oz) Chicken Stock
   (page 174)

1 bay leaf

1 cinnamon stick

6 black peppercorns

SALSA VERDE

1 cup firmly packed mixed fresh herbs,
   including flat-leaf (Italian) parsley, mint,
   basil, coriander (cilantro)

1 clove garlic, chopped

1 tsp capers

1 tsp gluten-free Dijon mustard

1 tbsp lemon juice

2 tbsp olive oil

To make Salsa Verde, combine all ingredients in a food processor and process until smooth. Season to taste.

Tie each piece of beef with string around the circumference to form a neat shape, leaving a loop of string, and bring to room temperature.

To make Poaching Stock, combine all ingredients in a large saucepan and bring to the boil, then reduce heat to a low simmer. Thread the loops of string over the handle of one or two wooden spoons and lower beef into poaching liquid, resting the spoons on the rim of the pan. The liquid should be just moving in the pan. Poach for 6 minutes for rare and 8 minutes for medium-rare. Remove from pan, remove string and wrap each piece of beef in plastic wrap and rest until ready to serve. Reserve stock.

Meanwhile, cook potatoes in simmering salted water until just tender. Coarsely mash potatoes, adding a little reserved poaching stock and season to taste.

Bring 2 cups (16 fl oz) reserved poaching stock to the boil and reduce by half. Whisk in mustard and season to taste.

To serve, place a scoop of potato in the centre of each shallow bowl. Slice each piece of beef in half and place on top of potato, then top with asparagus and a spoonful of Salsa Verde. Drizzle over reduced stock.

SERVES 4

Poaching stock can be prepared a day ahead.

GLUTEN-FREE ✔ **DAIRY-FREE** ✔

butterfly lamb with roasted red vegetables & warm mint sauce

You could use lamb rump from the chump end of the chops for this recipe but there will be a lot of fat that needs to be removed, which seems quite wasteful. The roasted red vegetables also team well with grilled chicken or quail.

2 kg (4 lb) leg of lamb, boned and butterflied, trimmed of fat olive oil

rocket (arugula) leaves, to serve

ROASTED RED VEGETABLES

4 baby beetroot (beets), trimmed

4 small carrots, trimmed

olive oil

2 Roma (plum) tomatoes, halved lengthwise

1 red capsicum (pepper), sliced lengthwise into 1 cm (^{1}/2 in) thick slices

1 red (Spanish) onion, cut into wedges

MINT SAUCE

^{1}/4 cup (2 fl oz) olive oil

1 eschalot (French shallot), finely chopped

1 cup firmly packed fresh mint leaves, chopped

^{1}/4 cup (2 fl oz) red wine vinegar

1 tsp gluten-free seeded mustard

To make Roasted Red Vegetables, wash beetroot, cover with foil and place on an oven tray. Cut carrots into 2 cm (^{3}/4 in) long pieces, toss with a little oil and place beside beetroot. Roast at 200°C (400°F) for 45–50 minutes or until beetroot and carrots are tender. Remove from oven. When cool enough to handle, peel beetroot and cut into wedges.

At the same time, place tomatoes, capsicum and onion on another tray, drizzle with 2 teaspoons oil and season to taste. Roast at 200°C (400°F) for 30 minutes or until capsicum and onion are browned. Gently toss tomato, capsicum and onion with beetroot and carrots.

Meanwhile, rub lamb with a little oil, place on an oven tray and roast shin-side up at 200°C (400°F) for 30–40 minutes for pink. Rest, loosely covered, in a warm place for 10 minutes.

To make Mint Sauce, combine all ingredients and season to taste. Place mint sauce in a saucepan and heat until just warm.

Place sliced lamb on rocket leaves and spoon warm sauce over. Serve roasted vegetables to one side.

SERVES 4

Best made just before serving.

GLUTEN-FREE ✓ DAIRY-FREE ✓ DETOX-FRIENDLY ✓ LUNCH BOX ✓

osso bucco with white bean mash

We have peeled the tomatoes for this dish but leave the skins if they don't bother you. Osso bucco is also delicious served with Soft Polenta (page 175) or plain steamed rice. Leave out the red wine and replace with stock if you prefer.

olive oil

1 onion, finely chopped

1 carrot, finely chopped

1 stick celery, finely chopped

4 large vine-ripened tomatoes, peeled, chopped

4 cloves garlic, chopped

1/2 cup (4 fl oz) dry red wine

1 cup (8 fl oz) Chicken Stock (page 174)

1 kg (2 lb) veal shanks, cut into 4 cm (1 1/2 in) thick pieces

2 tbsp chopped fresh flat-leaf (Italian) parsley

GREMOLATA

2 tsp grated lemon rind

2 cloves garlic, finely chopped

1/3 cup finely chopped fresh flat-leaf (Italian) parsley

WHITE BEAN MASH

1 tbsp olive oil

1 onion, finely chopped

1 clove garlic, chopped

3 x 400 g (13 oz) cans cannellini beans, drained and rinsed

2 tbsp Chicken Stock (page 174), approximately

2 tbsp lemon juice, or to taste

Heat 1 tablespoon oil in a large, heavy-based flameproof casserole dish and cook onion, carrot and celery, covered, over low heat until soft, adding a little of the stock if vegetables are sticking to pan. Add tomatoes and garlic and cook over high heat until tomatoes are thick and pulpy, then add wine and stock, bring to the boil and season to taste. Cook over high heat for 5 minutes.

Meanwhile, heat a little oil in a large non-stick frying pan and cook veal in batches over high heat on both sides until browned. Remove from pan and add to tomato mixture in casserole. Cover with a lid and bake at 180°C (350°F) for 1 1/2 hours or until veal is tender. Skim any fat from surface, stir in parsley and check seasoning.

To make Gremolata, combine all ingredients and mix well.

To make White Bean Mash, heat oil in a saucepan and cook onion and garlic over low heat until soft, adding a little water if sticking to pan. Add cannellini beans, stock and lemon juice and stir over medium heat for 2 minutes. Place mixture in a food processor and process until smooth, then season to taste, adding a little more stock or lemon juice if necessary. Return to pan and heat through.

Serve White Bean Mash topped with Osso Bucco and Gremolata.

SERVES 4

Osso bucco and mash can be prepared a day ahead.

grilled eggplant with pork & tofu

On its own, tofu can be quiet bland, but it is a wonderful carrier of flavours and, of course, it is very nutritious. We love it.
For a more substantial main course, serve this dish on a bed of rice noodles or with Steamed Ginger Rice (page 178).

1 X 500 g (1 lb) eggplant (aubergine),
  cut crosswise into 1 cm (1/2 in) thick
  slices

vegetable oil

600 g (1 lb 3 oz) pork fillet

6 eschalots (French shallots), sliced

3 small fresh red chillies, or to taste,
  sliced

3 cloves garlic, chopped

1 tbsp fish sauce

2 tsp grated palm sugar (jaggery) or
  brown sugar

1/4 cup (2 fl oz) wheat-free tamari sauce

2 tbsp lime juice

200 g (6 1/2 oz) firm tofu, cut into
  1 cm (1/2 in) pieces

300 g (10 oz) sugar snap peas, trimmed

100 g (3 1/2 oz) enoki mushrooms,
  trimmed

1 tbsp wheat-free tamari sauce, extra

1 tbsp shaohsing cooking wine

1 tbsp toasted sesame seeds

2 tbsp chopped toasted cashews

2 green (spring) onions (scallions), sliced

2 tbsp coriander (cilantro) leaves

lime wedges, to serve

Brush eggplant with a little oil and grill (broil) on both sides until golden.

Slice pork thinly across the grain. Heat 1 tablespoon oil in a wok and cook pork in batches over high heat until just cooked. Remove from wok and set aside.

Add another tablespoon of oil to wok, add eschalots and chillies and stir over high heat until golden. Add garlic, fish sauce, palm sugar, tamari, lime juice and tofu and stir to combine. Return pork to wok to heat through. Moisten with a little water if necessary. Remove from wok.

Meanwhile, heat 1 tablespoon oil in the wok and stir-fry sugar snap peas over high heat for 1 minute, then add mushrooms and stir for another minute. Add extra tamari and shaohsing cooking wine and stir to combine, then sprinkle with sesame seeds.

Serve eggplant topped with pork mixture, cashews, green onions and coriander. Serve with lime wedges and sugar snap pea mixture.

SERVES 4

Best made just before serving.

GLUTEN-FREE ✔ **DAIRY-FREE** ✔ **LUNCH BOX** ✔

pork vindaloo with spicy green beans

This is not an overwhelmingly hot curry, so if you want to increase the heat, simply up the number of dried chillies. You can also make this dish with beef. Ask your butcher for chuck steak, and get him to remove the fat.

4 small dried red chillies, crumbled

1 tsp cumin seeds

2 tsp black peppercorns

2 tbsp vegetable oil

2 onions, finely chopped

800 g (1 lb 10 oz) lean stewing pork, trimmed of fat and cut into 4 cm (1 1/2 in) pieces

1 tbsp finely grated fresh ginger

6 cloves garlic, crushed

1/2 tsp ground turmeric

1 cinnamon stick

3 fresh green chillies, sliced lengthwise

1 tsp salt

1/2 tsp tamarind concentrate

1/4 cup (2 fl oz) cider vinegar

1/2 tsp sugar

Steamed Ginger Rice (page 178), to serve

SPICY GREEN BEANS

500 g (1 lb) baby green beans, trimmed

1 tbsp vegetable oil

1 tsp black mustard seeds

2 small dried red chillies, crumbled

1/2 tsp ground turmeric

6 fresh curry leaves

1 tbsp grated fresh ginger

1 onion, chopped

1/4 cup (2 fl oz) lemon juice

Combine chillies, cumin seeds and peppercorns in a spice grinder and grind to a fine powder.

Heat oil in a large deep saucepan and cook onions, covered, over low heat until soft, adding a little water if sticking to pan. Add pork and spice mixture and stir over medium heat until pork is browned and spices are aromatic. Add ginger, garlic and turmeric and stir over heat for 1 minute. Cover pork with water, add cinnamon, green chillies and the salt and bring to the boil. Cook, partially covered, over low heat for 1 hour. Stir in tamarind, vinegar and sugar and cook, uncovered, for about 30 minutes or until sauce is thick.

To make Spicy Green Beans, cook beans in simmering salted water until just tender. Drain and rinse under cold water. Heat oil in a wok and stir mustard seeds over low heat until crackling. Add remaining ingredients, except lemon juice, and stir over medium heat until onion is soft, adding a little water if onion is sticking to the wok. Add beans and lemon juice, season with salt and cook until heated through.

Serve the pork with the beans and rice.

SERVES 4

Pork vindaloo can be prepared a day ahead.

GLUTEN-FREE ✔ **DAIRY-FREE** ✔

chargrilled tuna with eggplant jam

Eggplant jam is delicious and so easy to make. Serve as an accompaniment to lamb or chicken or as an appetiser, spread on Savoury Biscuits (page 149) or toasted gluten-free bread. Kingfish, snapper, blue eye or barramundi are also suitable for this recipe.

4 X 200 g (6½ oz) tuna steaks

olive oil

wilted spinach, to serve

Aioli (page 177), made with basil,
   to serve

small fresh basil leaves, to serve

EGGPLANT JAM

1 tbsp olive oil

½ onion, finely chopped

1 x 500 g (1 lb) eggplant (aubergine),
   chopped

3 cloves garlic, chopped

2 small fresh red chillies, or to taste,
   seeded, chopped

4 tomatoes, peeled, chopped

2 tbsp white wine vinegar

1 tbsp brown sugar

To make Eggplant Jam, heat oil in a large heavy-based saucepan and cook onion over low heat until soft. Add eggplant and stir over medium heat until browned. Add remaining ingredients and 1 cup (8 fl oz) water, bring to the boil, then cook over low heat for about 1 hour, stirring occasionally, until mixture is thick and pulpy, adding more water if necessary. Season to taste and cool.

Brush tuna with oil and chargrill for about 1 minute each side, depending on thickness, or until just cooked. Spoon wilted spinach onto plates and top with Eggplant Jam, tuna and a drizzle of Basil Aioli. Sprinkle with a few baby basil leaves.

SERVES 4

Makes about 3 cups (24 fl oz) eggplant jam

Eggplant jam can be made 3 days ahead.

crisp-skinned snapper with mussel & white bean ragout

The skin on snapper is delicious and also full of good nutrients. Sprinkle it with a little salt before you cook it and it will be even crispier. If you don't like the skin, ask your fishmonger to remove it. This recipe also works well with barramundi and salmon fillets.

½ cup (3½ oz) dried cannellini beans, soaked in cold water overnight, drained

1 eschalot (French shallot), finely chopped

¼ cup (2 fl oz) dry white wine or water

750 g (1½ lb) black mussels, scrubbed and bearded

pinch saffron threads, or to taste

olive oil

1 small onion, chopped

4 tomatoes, chopped

2 cloves garlic, chopped

1 cup (8 fl oz) Chicken Stock (page 174)

4 x 200 g (6½ oz) snapper fillets, skin on

sea salt

steamed asparagus, to serve

HERB SALAD

½ cup firmly packed fresh flat-leaf (Italian) parsley leaves

¼ cup firmly packed fresh coriander (cilantro) leaves

¼ cup firmly packed sprigs fresh dill

1 tbsp lemon juice

1 tbsp olive oil

Cook cannellini beans in simmering water for about 40 minutes or until tender. Drain.

Combine eschalot and wine or water in a shallow, wide pan and bring to the boil. Add mussels, cover, and cook over medium heat until mussels open. Remove mussels as they open and place in a bowl. Strain cooking juices and reserve. Add saffron. When mussels are cool enough to handle, remove mussel meat and discard shells.

Heat 1 tablespoon oil in a saucepan and cook onion over low heat until soft. Add tomatoes and garlic and cook over high heat until tomato is thick and pulpy. Add reserved mussel juice, stock and cannellini beans and simmer over low heat for 15 minutes. Add mussels and season to taste.

Meanwhile, brush snapper with a little oil and sprinkle skin with sea salt. Cook, skin side down, over high heat in a non-stick frying pan until skin is browned and crisp. Turn and cook over medium heat for about 2 minutes or until just cooked.

For Herb Salad, combine all ingredients and season to taste.

Spoon ragout into shallow bowls and top with snapper and Herb Salad. Serve with steamed asparagus on the side.

SERVES 4

Mussel & white bean ragout can be prepared 2 hours ahead.

seared salmon with stir-fried bok choy & tamari dressing

We have pan-fried the salmon in this recipe, but if you are wanting to reduce your fat intake, you could poach it instead. Salmon is such a versatile, nutritious fish and works well with most flavours.

2 green (spring) onions (scallions), trimmed to 6 cm (2 1/2 in), thinly sliced lengthwise

1 bunch broccolini, trimmed, halved lengthwise

grapeseed oil

4 baby bok choy (pak choy), trimmed

4 X 200 g (6 1/2 oz) salmon fillets, skinned

150 g (5 oz) rice noodles, cooked according to directions on packet

fresh coriander (cilantro) leaves, to serve

TAMARI DRESSING

4 green (spring) onions (scallions), finely chopped

3 cloves garlic, finely chopped

1 tsp grated fresh ginger

1 tbsp chopped fresh coriander (cilantro)

1/4 cup (2 fl oz) wheat-free tamari sauce

1 tbsp grapeseed oil

2 tsp sesame oil

1/4 cup (2 fl oz) lime juice

1/3 cup (2 1/2 fl oz) Chicken Stock (page 174)

1 small fresh red chilli, sliced (optional)

pinch of caster (superfine) sugar

To make Tamari Dressing, combine all ingredients and season to taste with sea salt and black pepper. Stand for 1 hour for flavours to develop and check seasoning again.

Place green onions in a bowl of chilled water and stand for 1 hour. Drain.

Add broccolini to a pan of simmering water and blanch for 1 minute. Drain and rinse under cold water.

Heat 2 teaspoons oil in a wok and stir-fry bok choy over high heat until just wilted. Add broccolini and stir-fry until heated through.

Meanwhile, brush salmon with a little oil and cook, skinned-side first, over high heat in a non-stick frying pan until browned and crisp. Turn and cook over medium heat for about 2 minutes or until just cooked.

Divide noodles among shallow bowls, top with bok choy mixture and drizzle with half the dressing. Top with salmon, green onions and coriander leaves and drizzle with remaining dressing.

SERVES 4

Dressing can be made 3 hours ahead.

GLUTEN-FREE ✓ **DAIRY-FREE** ✓ **DETOX-FRIENDLY** ✓

herb-crusted blue eye with cauliflower puree

Cauliflower might seem an unlikely mix with fish, but trust us, it works really well and can be seen on menus in combination with seafood in many Sydney restaurants. You can also use snapper for this recipe. Gluten-free breadcrumbs and bread are available from health food stores, some large supermarkets, or you can make our Yeast-free Hi-fibre Bread (page 146).

olive oil

1 cup chopped mixed fresh herbs including flat-leaf (Italian) parsley, dill, coriander (cilantro), mint

1 clove garlic, chopped

grated rind of 1 lemon

1 tbsp lemon juice

100 g (3 1/2 oz) fresh gluten-free breadcrumbs

4 X 200 g (6 1/2 oz) blue eye fillets, skinned

4 witlof (chicory/Belgian endive), halved lengthwise

2 tbsp balsamic vinegar

CAULIFLOWER PUREE

400 g (13 oz) cauliflower, trimmed

400 g (13 oz) Sebago potatoes, chopped

3 1/4 cups (26 fl oz) Chicken Stock (page 174)

Combine 1 tablespoon oil, herbs, garlic, lemon rind, lemon juice and breadcrumbs in a food processor, season, and process until ingredients come together in a paste.

Brush skinned side of fish with oil and top with herb mixture, pressing the mixture down onto fish. Place on an oven tray and roast at 220°C (425°F) for 7 minutes or until fish is just cooked and crust is browned. If crust is not brown enough, place under a hot grill (broiler) for a few seconds.

To make Cauliflower Puree, combine cauliflower, potatoes and stock in a saucepan and bring to the boil. Simmer over medium heat until cauliflower and potatoes are tender, then drain and reserve cooking liquid. Process cauliflower and potato with just enough reserved cooking liquid to form a smooth puree and season to taste.

Place witlof on an oven tray, brush with oil, season to taste and grill (broil) on both sides until browned and wilted.

Spoon Cauliflower Puree onto plates and top with fish. Serve witlof to one side, drizzled with balsamic vinegar.

SERVES 4

Best made just before serving.

flathead escabeche with aioli

Kathy first had escabeche on her travels in Portugal and Spain and fell in love with the flavours. A hot marinade is poured over the cooked fish then left to cool for the flavours to develop. You can also use this marinade to pour over cooked chicken or quail. This is a lovely dish to take on a picnic, as it can be prepared in advance.

olive oil

800 g (1 lb 10 oz) flathead fillets, cut into 8 cm (3 1/4 in) lengths

2 carrots, thinly sliced on the diagonal

1 red (Spanish) onion, halved, thinly sliced

1/2 tsp cumin seeds

1/2 tsp sweet paprika

pinch cayenne pepper, or to taste

2 bay leaves

6 sprigs fresh thyme

2 strips orange rind

1/4 cup (2 fl oz) sherry vinegar

1/4 cup (2 fl oz) orange juice

1 cup (8 fl oz) Chicken Stock (page 174)

2 cups baby spinach leaves

Aioli (page 177), to serve

steamed baby potatoes and sprigs fresh thyme, to serve

Heat a little oil in a non-stick frying pan and cook flathead in batches over medium heat until just cooked. Remove from pan and place in a glass or ceramic dish.

Add another splash of oil to pan and cook carrots, onion and cumin seeds over low heat until onion is soft, adding a little water if onion is sticking to pan. Add paprika, cayenne, bay leaves, thyme, orange rind, vinegar, juice and stock. Bring to the boil and simmer over medium heat until carrot is tender, then season to taste. Pour warm mixture over flathead and bring to room temperature.

Toss baby spinach leaves with a little oil and top with flathead mixture and a dollop of aioli. Serve with steamed potatoes tossed with sprigs of thyme.

SERVES 4

Flathead escabeche can be prepared 3 hours ahead.

GLUTEN-FREE ✔   DAIRY-FREE ✔   DETOX-FRIENDLY ✔   LUNCH BOX ✔

roasted baby bream with potato, garlic & radicchio

We have used individual fish for this recipe for ease of serving, but you can also put all the vegetables in one pan and roast a larger fish to serve four. Individual baby snapper work well in this dish too.

800 g (1 lb 10 oz) desiree potatoes, cut into wedges

1 X 500 g (1 lb) bulb fennel, trimmed, cut into wedges

olive oil

16 cloves garlic, skin on

4 x 400 g (13 oz) baby bream, cleaned and scaled

1/2 cup (4 fl oz) Chicken Stock (page 174) or dry white wine

4 vine-ripened tomatoes, peeled, seeded, chopped

1/2 cup (2 1/2 oz) kalamata olives

1 radicchio, outer leaves removed, quartered lengthwise

lemon wedges, to serve

Cook potato and fennel wedges separately in simmering salted water for 5 minutes, then drain.

Drizzle two roasting pans with a little oil, divide potato between pans and toss to coat with oil. Roast at 200°C (400°F) for 15 minutes, then add fennel and garlic cloves (dividing them between the pans) and roast for another 15 minutes. Remove from oven and turn with a spatula. Place two fish in each pan, sitting them on the vegetables, drizzle with stock or wine, then season to taste. Scatter tomatoes and olives over fish and roast for another 20 minutes or until fish is cooked. Remove from oven and rest in pan for 5 minutes.

Place radicchio quarters on an oven tray, brush with a little oil, season to taste and roast at 200°C (400°F) for 3–5 minutes, turning once, until softened and browned on the edges.

Serve fish on a bed of vegetables with roasted radicchio and lemon wedges to one side. Squeeze garlic out of its skin to eat with the fish.

SERVES 4

Best made just before serving.

GLUTEN-FREE ✔ **DAIRY-FREE** ✔ **DETOX-FRIENDLY** ✔

poached ocean trout with crisp potatoes & stemperata sauce

Stemperata is a traditional Sicilian sauce – this is our version. It is wonderful with fish and can also be served with salmon, tuna or swordfish. You will need a fish kettle to poach a whole fish, but you can also poach individual fillets if you aren't cooking for the masses.

2.5 kg (5 lb) whole ocean trout, cleaned, scaled, at room temperature

1 small onion, sliced

2 bay leaves

6 sprigs fresh parsley

6 black peppercorns

2 kg (4 lb) small kipfler or waxy salad potatoes, washed

olive oil

steamed green beans, to serve

STEMPERATA SAUCE

1/2 cup (4 fl oz) olive oil

4 sticks celery, finely chopped

1 small red (Spanish) onion, finely chopped

4 cloves garlic, finely chopped

1 cup (5 oz) green olives, pitted, coarsely chopped

1/2 cup (2 1/2 oz) baby capers

2/3 cup (2 1/2 oz) currants, plumped in a little hot water, drained

1/4 cup (2 fl oz) white wine vinegar

1 tbsp chopped fresh oregano

To make Stemperata Sauce, combine all ingredients in a saucepan and cook over medium heat until vinegar has evaporated, then season to taste.

Place rinsed fish on a rack in a fish kettle, cover with cold water, then add onion, bay leaves, parsley and peppercorns. Cover fish kettle with a lid, place over two burners on the cooktop and bring slowly to the boil (this will take about 15 minutes). As soon as water begins to bubble, turn off heat and remove lid. Leave fish to cook in poaching liquid. The trout is cooked when the dorsal fin (the large one along the backbone) comes out easily when pulled. A fish this size will take 1 hour to finish cooking once heat has been turned off.

Remove fish from poaching liquid and remove skin and surface bones. Leave head and tail intact if you intend to serve it whole.

Meanwhile, cook potatoes in simmering salted water until tender. Drain and place on two oven trays. Using a rolling pin, lightly crush potatoes so that they split open. Brush with oil and season to taste, then roast at 200°C (400°F) for 30 minutes, turning occasionally, or until potatoes are crisp and tender.

Serve portions of ocean trout on a bed of steamed green beans, topped with a spoonful of sauce, with crisp potatoes to one side.

SERVES 10-12

Sauce can be prepared 3 hours ahead.

GLUTEN-FREE ✔ DAIRY-FREE ✔ DETOX-FRIENDLY ✔

barramundi baked in banana leaves with cucumber salad & coconut rice

Banana leaves are available from Asian grocery stores. If you can't find them, simply wrap the fish in foil – it will serve the same purpose of steaming the fish as it bakes. Coconut rice can be served as an accompaniment to many Asian-style fish dishes.

4 x 200 g (6½ oz) barramundi fillets

4 banana leaves

1 tbsp lime juice

8 sprigs fresh coriander (cilantro)

COCONUT RICE

1 tbsp vegetable oil

1 onion, chopped

2 cloves garlic, chopped

1 cup (6½ oz) jasmine rice

200 ml (6½ fl oz) hot light
  coconut milk

CUCUMBER SALAD

1 stick celery, thinly sliced on the
  diagonal

1 Lebanese (small green) cucumber,
  thinly sliced on the diagonal

2 green (spring) onions (scallions),
  sliced on the diagonal

1 baby bok choy (pak choy), thinly
  sliced lengthwise

¼ cup fresh coriander (cilantro) leaves

¼ cup fresh mint leaves

1 tbsp wheat-free tamari sauce

1 tbsp lime juice

To make Coconut Rice, heat oil in a saucepan and cook onion and garlic, covered, over low heat until onion is soft. Add rice, season with salt and stir to coat. Add hot coconut milk and 300 ml (10 fl oz) hot water, stir to combine and bring to the boil. Cover and cook over low heat for 10 minutes. Remove from heat and stand for 5 minutes before stirring with a fork. Check seasoning.

To make Cucumber Salad, combine all ingredients and toss gently.

Meanwhile, place barramundi fillets in centre of banana leaves, brush with lime juice and top each fillet with 2 sprigs of coriander. Wrap leaves around fish and place on an oven tray. Bake at 200°C (400°F) for 8–10 minutes, depending on the thickness, or until fish is just cooked. Stand fish for 5 minutes before removing banana leaf and serving.

Serve barramundi on a bed of coconut rice with the salad spooned over.

SERVES 4

Best made just before serving.

roasted kingfish with spinach, lentils & slow-roasted tomatoes

The little green lentils used in this dish are now grown in Australia and have a wonderful earthy, almost nutty flavour. If you can't get kingfish, snapper would work fine. You could also serve this lentil mixture with grilled trout or salmon.

4 Roma (plum) tomatoes, quartered lengthwise, halved crosswise
olive oil
1 cup (6½ oz) French-style green lentils
1 bunch spinach, trimmed
2 leeks, trimmed, chopped
2 tsp chopped fresh dill
4 x 200 g (6½ oz) kingfish fillets, skinned
1 tbsp lemon juice
1 tbsp sprigs fresh dill, extra

Place tomatoes on an oven tray, brush lightly with oil, season and roast at 100°C (200°F) for 1 hour.

Cook lentils in simmering water for about 20 minutes or until tender, then drain and rinse under cold water.

Wash spinach, place in a saucepan, cover and cook over medium heat until just wilted. Drain and rinse under cold water. When cool enough to handle press out excess water and chop coarsely.

Heat 1 tablespoon oil in a saucepan and cook leeks over low heat until soft, adding a little water if leeks are sticking to pan. Add spinach, lentils and dill, season to taste and stir over low heat until warm.

Brush skinned side of kingfish with oil and cook, skinned-side down, over high heat in a non-stick frying pan until browned, then place on an oven tray, cooked-side up, and roast at 200°C (400°F) for about 5 minutes or until just cooked.

Combine tomatoes, lemon juice and extra dill and toss gently. Serve kingfish on a bed of lentil mixture, topped with roasted tomato mixture.

SERVES 4

Lentil mixture can be prepared 1 hour ahead.

GLUTEN-FREE ✔ **DAIRY-FREE** ✔ **DETOX-FRIENDLY** ✔

goan fish stew with vegetable salad

This recipe has been adapted from Jan's book, Indian Home Cooking, which she co-wrote with Ajoy Joshi. This dish is hot, so cut back on the dried chillies if you have a delicate palate. The vegetable salad makes a lovely cooling accompaniment.

2 tbsp dried red chillies, broken into
  small pieces
2 tbsp coriander seeds
1 tbsp cumin seeds
1/3 cup (2 1/2 fl oz) white vinegar
2 tsp grated fresh ginger
4 cloves garlic, chopped
1 tsp ground turmeric
2 tbsp vegetable oil
2 onions, halved, sliced
1 large tomato, chopped
2 large fresh green chillies, halved lengthwise
1 1/4 cups (10 fl oz) light coconut milk
800 g (1 lb 10 oz) blue eye or ling
  fillets, or any firm white fish, cut into
  3 cm (1 1/4 in) pieces
Steamed Ginger Rice (page 178), to serve

VEGETABLE SALAD

1 onion, finely chopped
2 carrots, coarsely grated
1/2 cup fresh coriander (cilantro) leaves
2 tsp grated fresh ginger
2 tbsp chopped toasted unsalted peanuts or
  almonds
1/4 cup (2 fl oz) lemon juice

To make Vegetable Salad, combine all ingredients and season to taste.

Using a spice grinder or mortar and pestle, grind dried chillies, coriander and cumin seeds into a powder. Transfer to a bowl, add vinegar, ginger, garlic and turmeric and stir to form a paste.

Heat oil in a large saucepan and cook onions, covered, over low heat until soft. Add spice paste and stir over low heat for about 3 minutes or until fragrant. Add tomato, fresh chillies and coconut milk and cook over low heat for 5 minutes, then season to taste with salt. Add fish and cook over low heat for about 5 minutes or until fish is just cooked.

Serve stew with Vegetable Salad and Steamed Ginger Rice.

SERVES 4

Best made just before serving.

GLUTEN-FREE ✔ DAIRY-FREE ✔ LUNCH BOX ✔

seared jewfish with harissa dressing

Harissa is a fiery Middle Eastern chilli paste, which can be used in a number of ways. You can stir it into soups, add it to sauces or, as we have done here, add it to yoghurt to form a dressing. If jewfish is not available, substitute with snapper or salmon – we have tried it with both.

1 red capsicum (pepper), sliced

4 zucchini (courgettes), sliced lengthwise
   into 8 pieces

1 red (Spanish) onion, cut into 8 wedges

olive oil

4 x 200 g (6½ oz) jewfish fillets, skinned

fresh coriander (cilantro) leaves

steamed kipfler or waxy salad potatoes
   and Leafy Green Salad (page 176),
   to serve

HARISSA DRESSING

2–3 tbsp Harissa (page 177), or to taste

½ cup (4 fl oz) plain soy yoghurt

To make Harissa Dressing, combine harissa and yoghurt and season to taste.

Combine capsicum, zucchini and onion in a shallow roasting pan, toss with 1 tablespoon oil and season to taste. Roast at 200°C (400°F) for 30 minutes, turning occasionally, until vegetables are tender and browned.

Heat 1 tablespoon oil in a non-stick frying pan and cook fish over high heat on one side until golden, then turn and cook over medium heat until cooked to your liking.

Spread a little of the dressing on each serving plate and top with capsicum mixture and fish. Spoon a dollop of remaining dressing over the fish and sprinkle with coriander leaves. Serve with potatoes and a green salad.

SERVES 4

Dressing can be prepared a day ahead.

GLUTEN-FREE ✔   DAIRY-FREE ✔   DETOX-FRIENDLY ✔

swordfish kebabs with shaved fennel & broadbean salad

If large fennel bulbs are not in season, you can substitute two baby fennel bulbs. These are grown in hot houses and are available all year round in some areas. Preparing artichokes is a bit of a process. If you don't have the time, look for prepared grilled artichokes in delicatessens. This is a light dish, and is also good for picnics.

1 X 400 g (13 oz) bulb fennel, trimmed, halved lengthwise, cored

1 kg (2 lb) broadbeans (fava beans), podded

2 globe artichokes

lemon juice

extra virgin olive oil

8 slices prosciutto, trimmed of fat

800 g (1 lb 10 oz) piece swordfish, cut into 3 cm (1 1/4 in) pieces

4 bamboo skewers, soaked in cold water for 30 minutes

2 cups trimmed watercress

lemon wedges, to serve

Slice fennel thinly with a mandolin and place in a bowl of cold water for 30 minutes. Drain and pat dry with paper towel.

Cook broadbeans in simmering salted water for 2 minutes. Drain, rinse under cold water and remove shells.

Trim artichoke leaves and stems and cut artichokes in half. Remove and discard hairy choke and place artichoke immediately in a bowl of water with a little lemon juice added.

When both artichokes are prepared, cook in simmering salted water until tender. Drain, remove excess outer leaves and halve lengthwise again. Brush artichokes with a little oil and chargrill over high heat until browned, then season to taste.

Halve prosciutto lengthwise and wrap around each piece of swordfish. Thread swordfish onto skewers and brush with a little oil. Chargrill or grill (broil) swordfish kebabs over medium heat for about 2 minutes each side, which will leave them a little rare in the centre, or cook to your liking.

Combine watercress, fennel, broadbeans, 1 tablespoon lemon juice and 2 tablespoons oil, season to taste and toss gently. Place kebabs on a bed of fennel salad, top with grilled artichokes and serve with lemon wedges.

SERVES 4

Artichokes can be prepared a day ahead.

rice noodle pancakes with tofu & eggplant

These pancakes can be made in varying sizes to suit the occasion. If you make tiny ones, serve them topped with the Avocado & Mango Salsa as an appetiser. For a special treat, top the salsa with a few salmon pearls (salmon caviar).

6 baby eggplant (aubergine), halved lengthwise

grapeseed oil

sea salt

200 g (6 1/2 oz) firm tofu, drained, chopped into 2 cm (3/4 in) pieces

fresh coriander (cilantro) leaves, to serve

RICE NOODLE PANCAKES

50 g (1 3/4 oz) rice vermicelli noodles

1/2 sheet nori (seaweed)

150 ml (5 fl oz) light coconut milk

1/4 cup (1 1/4 oz) rice flour

2 egg whites

grapeseed oil

AVOCADO & MANGO SALSA

1 small avocado, chopped

1/2 mango, finely chopped

1/4 small red (Spanish) onion, finely chopped

1 tbsp chopped fresh coriander (cilantro)

1 small tomato, seeded, finely chopped

1 small fresh red chilli, finely chopped

1 tbsp lime juice

1 tbsp extra virgin olive oil

To make Rice Noodle Pancakes, soak noodles in boiling water for 5 minutes. Drain well, pat dry with paper towel and chop coarsely. Dip nori briefly in hot water, then drain and chop.

Combine coconut milk and rice flour in a bowl and mix well. Stir in noodles and nori and generously season to taste. Whisk egg whites until soft peaks form, then fold into noodle mixture in two batches.

Heat a little oil in a non-stick frying pan and cook scant 1/4 cupfuls of mixture in batches until golden, then turn and cook other side. Drain on paper towel.

To make Avocado & Mango Salsa, combine all ingredients and season to taste.

Brush eggplant with oil, sprinkle with sea salt, place on an oven tray and grill (broil) until golden, then turn and grill the other side, if necessary. Brush tofu with oil, sprinkle with sea salt and stir-fry in a non-stick frying pan in batches until golden.

Serve pancakes topped with eggplant, tofu, the salsa and coriander leaves.

SERVES 4

Makes 8 pancakes

Best made just before serving.

GLUTEN-FREE ✔ DAIRY-FREE ✔ DETOX-FRIENDLY ✔

baked pumpkin 'gnocchi' with roasted tomatoes & salsa verde

Pumpkin is such a delicious vegetable and jap is a sweet and creamy variety, ideal for baking. This dish was a favourite of one of our friends, Bronwen, who gave us a hand with some of the recipe testing. You could also top the 'gnocchi' with Mushroom Ragout & Roasted Zucchini Flowers (page 75)

1 kg (2 lb) jap pumpkin (squash), skin on, cut into chunks

olive oil

100 g (3 1/2 oz) firm tofu, well drained, chopped

2 eggs

100 g (3 1/2 oz) chickpea (besan) flour

2 bunches English spinach, trimmed, washed

1 small onion, finely chopped

2 cloves garlic, chopped

Slow-roasted Tomatoes (page 177), to serve

Olive & Thyme Focaccia (page 148), to serve

SALSA VERDE

1 cup chopped mixed fresh herbs, including basil, flat-leaf (Italian) parsley, dill, mint

1 tsp gluten-free Dijon mustard

2 cloves garlic, chopped

2 tbsp lemon juice

2 tbsp olive oil

To make Salsa Verde, combine all ingredients in a food processor, season to taste and process until smooth.

Place pumpkin, skin-side down, on an oven tray. Brush with oil, season and roast at 200°C (400°F) for 30–40 minutes or until pumpkin is soft. Remove from oven and use a spoon to scoop out pumpkin flesh.

Combine pumpkin flesh, tofu and eggs in a food processor and process until smooth. Stir in flour and season to taste. Brush a 20 cm (8 in) square cake tin with oil and line base with baking paper. Spoon pumpkin mixture into tin and bake at 180°C (350°F) for 20 minutes or until firm. Remove from oven and stand in tin for 10 minutes. Run a knife around edge of mixture and turn out onto a flat surface. Cut into 4 squares, then each square into 4 pieces.

Place spinach in a saucepan, cover and cook over medium heat until just wilted. Drain and squeeze out excess water. Heat 1 tablespoon oil in a frying pan and cook onion over low heat until soft. Add wilted spinach and garlic, season to taste and stir over low heat until warm.

Divide pumpkin 'gnocchi' among bowls and serve topped with spinach mixture, warm roasted tomatoes and salsa verde. Serve with gluten-free focaccia.

SERVES 4

Best made just before serving.

GLUTEN-FREE ✔   DAIRY-FREE ✔   DETOX-FRIENDLY ✔   LUNCH BOX ✔

vegetable biryani with pumpkin dahl

Biryani is spicy rather than hot, and we have left it that way. If you wish to add more heat to the dish, put more chilli powder in the pumpkin dahl.

½ cup (3½ oz) dried chickpeas,
  soaked in cold water overnight

2 tbsp vegetable oil

1 onion, sliced

4 cardamom pods, crushed

3 cloves

1 cinnamon stick

1 tsp cumin seeds

3 cloves garlic, chopped

1 tbsp grated fresh ginger

½ tsp ground turmeric

1 tsp ground coriander

pinch saffron threads, or to taste

2 bay leaves

1 carrot, chopped

1 potato, chopped

100 g (3½ oz) green beans,
  trimmed, halved

2 tomatoes, chopped

200 g (6½ oz) basmati rice

¼ cup (1½ oz) sultanas

toasted flaked almonds and
  fresh coriander (cilantro) leaves

Pumpkin dahl (page 178)

Cook drained chickpeas in simmering water for 45 minutes or until tender. Drain.

Heat oil in a large saucepan, add onion and cook over low heat until golden. Add cardamom, cloves, cinnamon, cumin seeds, garlic, ginger, turmeric and ground coriander and cook over low heat for 1 minute, adding a little water if sticking to pan.

Add saffron, bay leaves, vegetables and ½ cup (4 fl oz) water, then cover and cook over medium heat for 15 minutes, adding more water if necessary, or until vegetables are tender. Add chickpeas, rice, sultanas, salt to taste and 1½ cups (12 fl oz) hot water and bring to the boil, then cover and cook over very low heat for 10 minutes. Remove from heat, stand covered for another 10 minutes, then fluff with a fork.

Spoon biryani into bowls, top with toasted almonds and coriander leaves, and serve with the dahl.

SERVES 4–6

Dahl can be prepared a day ahead.

GLUTEN-FREE ✔   **DAIRY-FREE** ✔   **DETOX-FRIENDLY** ✔   **LUNCH BOX** ✔

tomato rice with roasted garlic & white bean puree

You can use any kind of dried bean in this paella-style dish, or substitute the dried beans with chicken or seafood if you are not looking for a vegetarian dish. You can also serve the puree as a topping for bread or biscuits, or with crudités.

½ cup (3½ oz) dried kidney beans, soaked in cold water overnight

1 tbsp olive oil

1 onion, chopped

1 carrot, finely chopped

1 stick celery, finely chopped

4 cups (32 fl oz) hot Vegetable Stock (page 174), approximately

3 cloves garlic, chopped

5 large vine-ripened tomatoes, peeled, seeded, chopped

½ tsp sweet paprika

2 bay leaves

½ tsp saffron threads, soaked in 1 tbsp hot water for 10 minutes

1 ½ cups (10 oz) Calasparra or arborio rice

200 g (6½ oz) flat Roman beans, trimmed, cut into 4 cm (1½ in) lengths

Leafy Green Salad (page 176), to serve

ROASTED GARLIC & WHITE BEAN PUREE

½ cup (3½ oz) cannellini beans, soaked in cold water overnight, drained

1 head garlic

2 tbsp lemon juice, or to taste

1 tbsp olive oil

To make Roasted Garlic & White Bean Puree, cook drained canellini beans in simmering salted water for about 45 minutes or until soft. Drain.

Place whole garlic head on an oven tray and roast at 200°C (400°F) for 30 minutes or until garlic is soft. When cool enough to handle, squeeze out garlic. Combine garlic, cooked beans and remaining ingredients in a food processor and process until smooth, then season to taste.

Cook drained kidney beans in simmering water for about 45 minutes or until tender, then drain.

Heat oil in a 34 cm (13½ in) paella pan and cook onion, carrot and celery over low heat until soft, adding a little stock if onion is sticking to pan. Add garlic, tomatoes, paprika, bay leaves and saffron mixture and cook over high heat until tomatoes are thick and pulpy. Add rice and stir to coat with tomato mixture. Add 1 cup (8 fl oz) hot stock to pan and cook over high heat for 5 minutes to create a crust on bottom of pan. Add three-quarters of remaining stock, kidney beans and Roman beans and season to taste. Do not stir.

Cook over medium heat for another 20 minutes or until rice is cooked and stock is absorbed, adding more stock if necessary. The rice should be quite dry. Remove from heat and cover with a clean tea towel for 10 minutes before serving. Serve topped with a dollop of bean puree, with a green salad.

SERVES 4–6

Best made just before serving.

GLUTEN-FREE ✔   DAIRY-FREE ✔   DETOX-FRIENDLY ✔   LUNCH BOX ✔

stir-fried tofu & vegetables with coriander & garlic

Stir-fries can get a bit out of hand, sometimes ending up with all the leftovers from the refrigerator thrown in. We like to be a bit more thoughtful about what we add – this dish has strong flavours and you can taste all the components.

vegetable oil

4 eschalots (French shallots), sliced

¾ cup firmly packed fresh coriander (cilantro) stems and leaves

6 cloves garlic, chopped

1 small onion, halved, sliced

½ red capsicum (pepper), chopped

2 baby bok choy (pak choy), trimmed, chopped into 3 cm (1 ¼ in) pieces

25 g (1 oz) dried shiitake mushrooms, soaked in hot water for 30 minutes, drained

100 g (3½ oz) snowpeas (mangetout), trimmed

200 g (6½ oz) tofu, cut into 2 cm (¾ in) pieces

2 tbsp fish sauce

2 tbsp wheat-free tamari sauce

150 g (5 oz) rice noodles, cooked according to directions on packet

lime wedges, to serve

Heat 2 tablespoons oil in a non-stick wok and cook eschalots over medium-high heat until golden and crisp. Drain on paper towel.

Combine coriander, garlic and 1 tablespoon oil in the small bowl of a food processor and process until mixture forms a paste.

Heat 2 tablespoons oil in the wok and cook coriander paste over low heat for 5–10 minutes or until fragrant. Add onion and capsicum and stir-fry for about 2 minutes. Add bok choy, mushrooms, snowpeas and tofu and stir-fry for another 2 minutes. Add fish sauce and tamari and stir-fry for another minute.

Place stir-fry on a bed of rice noodles, top with crisp eschalots, and serve with lime wedges to one side.

SERVES 4

Best made just before serving.

sweet potato frittata
with walnut & herb salsa

The Walnut and Herb Salsa is one of our favourites and is very versatile. It works just as well served with this frittata as it does with lamb or seafood. You could add other vegetables to the frittata, but we like to keep the flavours simple.

500 g (1 lb) desiree potatoes, halved

500 g (1 lb) orange sweet potato, peeled, cut into 3 cm (1 1/4 in) long pieces

8 eggs, lightly whisked

1 red capsicum (pepper), roasted, peeled, sliced

1/4 cup (1 oz) pitted black olives, halved

olive oil

Rocket & Pear Salad (page 175), to serve

WALNUT & HERB SALSA

50 g (1 3/4 oz) walnuts, toasted

4 green (spring) onions (scallions), chopped

2 cloves garlic, chopped

1 tsp gluten-free Dijon mustard

1/4 cup chopped fresh coriander (cilantro)

1/4 cup chopped fresh flat-leaf (Italian) parsley

2 tbsp lemon juice

1/4 cup (2 fl oz) extra virgin olive oil

To make Walnut & Herb Salsa, combine all ingredients and season to taste

Cook potatoes and sweet potato separately in simmering salted water for 15–20 minutes or until tender. Drain and cut both into 5 mm (1/4 in) thick slices.

Place eggs in a large bowl and season. Stir in potato, sweet potato, capsicum and olives. Lightly grease a 28 cm (11 1/4 in) non-stick frying pan with oil, add potato mixture, then cook over low-medium heat for about 5 minutes or until base is browned. Place under a medium grill (broiler) and cook until frittata is just set and top is golden. Stand in pan for 10 minutes, then run a knife around the edge and turn out onto a serving plate.

Serve wedges of frittata topped with the salsa, with Rocket & Pear Salad alongside.

SERVES 4

Best made just before serving.

GLUTEN-FREE ✔ DAIRY-FREE ✔ DETOX-FRIENDLY ✔ LUNCH BOX ✔

moroccan lentil soup

This hearty soup is a satisfying meal in itself – it needs no accompaniment, although you could follow it with Baby Spinach & Pomegranate Seed Salad (page 176). The soup thickens on standing, so if you are making it the day before you might need to add a little water when reheating, and check the seasoning.

½ cup (3½ oz) dried chickpeas, soaked in cold water overnight, drained

½ cup (3½ oz) dried haricot beans, soaked in cold water overnight, drained

½ cup (3½ oz) red lentils

1 tbsp olive oil

1 onion, chopped

4 cloves garlic, chopped

400 g (13 oz) can peeled chopped tomatoes

good pinch saffron threads, or to taste

⅓ cup (2½ fl oz) lemon juice

⅓ cup (2 oz) long-grain rice, cooked

1 tbsp chopped fresh coriander (cilantro)

1 tbsp chopped fresh flat-leaf (Italian) parsley

1 tbsp chopped fresh mint

1 tbsp Harissa (page 177), or to taste, to serve

Cook chickpeas and haricot beans in 1.5 litres (48 fl oz) simmering water for about 40 minutes or until just tender. Add lentils and continue cooking until lentils are soft.

Meanwhile, heat oil in a large saucepan and cook onion over low heat until soft. Add garlic and tomatoes and cook over high heat until tomatoes are thick and pulpy. Add saffron, lemon juice and 2 cups (16 fl oz) water, bring to the boil and simmer for 5 minutes. Add chickpea mixture, season to taste and simmer for another 20 minutes. Stir in rice and herbs and cook until rice is heated through.

Serve soup topped with a small spoonful of harissa to stir in.

SERVES 4–6

Soup can be prepared a day ahead.

GLUTEN-FREE ✔ DAIRY-FREE ✔ DETOX-FRIENDLY ✔ LUNCH BOX ✔

warm corn and borlotti bean salad with avocado dressing

If fresh borlotti beans are in season (summer), you can use those instead of dried ones, but the cooking time will be shorter. You could also add leftover chicken, lamb or beef to this salad if you are not planning a vegetarian meal.

1 cup (6½ oz) dried borlotti beans, soaked in cold water overnight, drained

2 tbsp red wine vinegar

2 tbsp olive oil

2 tbsp chopped fresh chives

100 g (3½ oz) cherry tomatoes, halved

2 corn cobs

175 g (5¾ oz) baby beans, trimmed

2 cups baby spinach leaves

extra fresh chives, to serve

AVOCADO DRESSING

½ avocado

1 clove garlic, chopped

2 tbsp lemon juice

2 tbsp olive oil

To make Avocado Dressing, combine all ingredients in a food processor and process until smooth, then season to taste.

Cook borlotti beans in simmering water for about 45 minutes or until tender. Drain. Combine borlotti beans, vinegar, oil and chives and season to taste.

Place tomatoes on an oven tray, brush with oil, season and roast at 180°C (350°F) for 20 minutes.

Meanwhile, remove kernels from corn and cook in simmering salted water for 30 seconds, then drain and rinse under cold water and add to borlotti mixture.

Cook baby beans in simmering salted water for 3 minutes, then drain and rinse under cold water.

Divide spinach among plates and top with borlotti mixture. Top with beans and tomatoes and a dollop of the dressing. Sprinkle with extra chives and serve.

SERVES 4

Best made just before serving.

GLUTEN-FREE ✓ DAIRY-FREE ✓ DETOX-FRIENDLY ✓ LUNCH BOX ✓

dessert

JAN: *I always have fresh fruit after dinner when dining at home and this varies depending on the seasons. On hot summer days I definitely enjoy having something cooling like our Mango Sorbet (page 131) or the Pineapple, Ginger & Lemongrass Granita (page 134), usually with some fruit. When we entertain, I like to think of dessert first and then plan the meal around it (I do that when I go out for dinner too). I have found that very rich desserts don't sit well if the previous courses are on the filling side, so I might go for something quite light, or share a dessert when dining out. One of my favourites is Black Sticky Rice (page 135) because I adore Asian desserts.*

KATHY: *Being part owner of the Sydney-based bakery Manna From Heaven means that I am surrounded by gorgeous little cakes that are ideal to serve as dessert, particularly if I am in a hurry. We make a gluten-free lemon polenta cake, which is our biggest seller, as well as chocolate raspberry brownies, hazelnut praline cakes, vanilla cakes and more. Generally, during the week I don't bother with a dessert and like to keep the evening meal light. However, I will always make a dessert if I am entertaining or if I feel like indulging on the weekend. I love fruit-based desserts, and anything with lemon, like our Lemon & Lime Delicious (page 141).*

We have included very luscious, indulgent desserts for special occasions and some lighter desserts to enjoy more often. You will find recipes like Almond Meringue Cake with Almond Cream (page x) which is wonderful for entertaining, a lovely moist Steamed Sago Plum Pudding (page 130) for Christmas (or anytime really) and a terrific Old-fashioned Trifle (page 139) that has guests asking for seconds. Of course, all the recipes are gluten- and dairy-free, which makes entertaining that much easier. We have mentioned in the recipe introductions if the dessert is a little high in fat and sugar, as a guide. To help maintain a healthy weight, it is best to have fresh fruit or a light fruit dessert the majority of the time if you enjoy something sweet after dinner. Just occasionally enjoy something a little richer and don't forget to balance it out over the day by having lighter meals.

almond meringue cake with almond cream

Kathy developed this recipe for a gluten-free feature she was writing for 'Cuisine' magazine. It's quite decadent and while it is easy to make, you should probably reserve it for special occasions (if you are watching your waistline), rather than everyday fare.

100 g (3½ oz) blanched almonds

4 egg whites

250 g (8 oz) caster (superfine) sugar

½ tsp vanilla extract

½ tsp white vinegar

200 g (6½ oz) dark chocolate, chopped

ALMOND CREAM

200 g (6½ oz) almond meal

60 g (2 oz) plain soy yoghurt

1 tbsp honey

Place blanched almonds on an oven tray and toast at 180°C (350°F) for 15 minutes or until golden. Cool, then process in a food processor until coarsely ground.

Using electric beaters, whisk egg whites until stiff. Gradually whisk in sugar, vanilla and vinegar until egg whites are very stiff. Use a large metal spoon to fold in the almonds.

Draw two 20 cm (8 in) circles on two pieces of baking paper. Place paper on two oven trays and spoon meringue mixture onto the circles, smoothing evenly with a spatula. Bake at 180°C (350°F) for 35 minutes, covering with foil if browning, or until firm to touch. Cool and remove paper.

To make Almond Cream, place almond meal, yoghurt and honey in a bowl and whisk together until well combined, adding ½ cup (4 fl oz) water, or just enough to form a thick cream that holds its shape.

Place chocolate in a heatproof bowl over a saucepan of simmering water and stir until just melted.

Sandwich meringue discs with almond cream. Cut into wedges and serve immediately drizzled with hot melted chocolate.

SERVES 8

Almond cream can be made a day ahead. Keep in an airtight container in refrigerator. Dessert can be made and assembled 3 hours ahead.

GLUTEN-FREE ✔ **DAIRY-FREE** ✔

mango sorbet with summer fruit salsa

This dessert is wonderful because it looks and tastes very special but there's absolutely no added sugar or fat, which makes it quite suitable for a nightly treat. It's one of Jan's favourite desserts for summer when mangoes are at their best. Choose an apple juice without preservatives or make your own if you have a juice extractor (use sweet red apples, not green).

1 kg (2 lb) ripe mangoes, peeled and flesh cut from seeds

1 cup (8 fl oz) unsweetened 100% apple juice

1 egg white

SUMMER FRUIT SALSA

1 ripe peach, halved, finely diced

1 ripe mango, cheeks removed, peeled, finely diced

100 g (3 1/2 oz) berries, such as blueberries, raspberries or chopped strawberries

2 passionfruit

Place mango flesh and apple juice in the bowl of a food processor and process until smooth. (Alternatively, use a hand-blender). Spoon into a non-aluminium freezer container and freeze, stirring once or twice, for 8 hours or until just frozen.

Whisk egg white in a small bowl until firm peaks form. Break up frozen mango mixture and place in the bowl of a food processor. Process, occasionally scraping down bowl with spatula, until smooth. Add egg white and process until combined. Return mixture to the freezer container and freeze overnight.

To make Summer Fruit Salsa, combine peach, mango, berries and passionfruit pulp in a bowl and mix gently.

Before serving, remove sorbet from freezer and place in refrigerator for 10 minutes to soften slightly. Spoon the fruit salsa into serving bowls or glasses and use an ice-cream scoop to place a large scoop of sorbet on top. Serve immediately.

SERVES 6

Sorbet can be made up to 2 weeks ahead. Keep in freezer. Fruit Salsa is best made on day of serving. Keep in airtight container in refrigerator.

GLUTEN-FREE ✔ DAIRY-FREE ✔ DETOX-FRIENDLY ✔

chocolate hazelnut cake with strawberry compote

This is a lovely cake to serve at dinner parties or at parties. It is moist, nutty and decadent and, best of all, easy to make. We recommend that you indulge in this cake only occasionally, as it is quite high in fat and sugar.

200 g (6 1/2 oz) hazelnuts

macadamia oil, to grease

3/4 cup (2 1/2 oz) cocoa powder

1 tbsp very strong black coffee

3/4 cup (5 oz) caster (superfine) sugar

6 eggs, separated

STRAWBERRY COMPOTE

250 g (8 oz) fresh strawberries, hulled, finely diced

2 tbsp sweet white wine, verjuice and vanilla bean syrup or Frangelico liqueur

Spread hazelnuts on an oven tray and toast at 180°C (350°F) for 5–7 minutes or until lightly browned and aromatic. Place nuts in a clean tea towel and rub to remove skins. Place skinned nuts in a food processor and process until finely ground.

Brush a round 22 cm (8 1/2 in) cake pan with oil to lightly grease. Line the base with baking paper.

Combine cocoa powder and 2/3 cup (5 fl oz) hot water in a mixing bowl and mix until smooth. Stir in the hazelnuts, coffee, sugar and egg yolks. Mix well.

Use an electric beater to whisk egg whites in a clean bowl until soft peaks form. Use a large metal spoon to fold a spoonful of egg whites into the cocoa mixture until combined, then gently fold in remaining egg whites until combined.

Pour cake mixture into prepared pan and place the pan in a roasting pan. Pour enough boiling water into the roasting pan to come halfway up the side of the cake pan. Bake in 180°C (350°F) oven for 40 minutes or until a skewer inserted in the centre of the cake comes out clean (the skewer will be a little sticky because the cake is moist).

Remove cake pan from water bath and set aside for 20 minutes to cool slightly. Turn onto a wire rack and remove paper. Cool to room temperature before placing on a serving plate.

To make Strawberry Compote, combine the strawberries and wine, syrup or liqueur in a bowl and mix well. Place in refrigerator for an hour or so to macerate.

Cut cake into wedges and place on serving plates. Serve with the strawberry compote.

SERVES 8

The cake keeps well in an airtight container for up to 3 days. Strawberry compote can be made several hours ahead and kept, covered, in refrigerator

GLUTEN-FREE ✔ **DAIRY-FREE** ✔

pineapple, ginger & lemongrass granita

Use a very sweet pineapple such as the bethonga variety. This granita is ideal to serve on a hot day as it is very refreshing and cooling. If you like, serve with fresh fruit.

850 ml (27 fl oz) can unsweetened
   pineapple juice

1/2 cup (3 1/2 oz) sugar

1 tbsp finely chopped fresh ginger

2 stems lemongrass, pale section
   finely chopped

1 kg (2 lb) pineapple, rind removed,
   quartered, cored and roughly chopped

Combine pineapple juice, sugar, ginger and lemongrass in a saucepan. Bring to the boil, stirring, over medium-high heat. Reduce heat to medium and cook, uncovered, for 20 minutes or until reduced a little. Set aside to cool.

Process pineapple in a food processor until pureed. Pour into a large bowl. Strain juice mixture into pureed pineapple and mix well. Pour into a shallow airtight container and freeze for 3 hours or until partially frozen. Use a fork to break up the frozen sections and stir well. Cover and freeze for a further 3 hours, then use the fork to break up the crystals and stir well. Cover and freeze overnight.

Remove from the freezer just before serving and use a strong fork to scrape the mixture into ice crystals. Serve in chilled glasses or bowls.

SERVES 6–8

Granita can be made 1 week ahead. Cover tightly and keep in freezer.

GLUTEN-FREE ✔ **DAIRY-FREE** ✔

black sticky rice with coconut cream

This recipe was inspired by Jan's recent holiday to Bali where she visited the Casa Luna cooking school in Ubud. Pandan leaves give a unique flavour to the dessert. You can find them in the freezer section of your Asian supermarket. If they are not available, use pandan essence or omit entirely. We would serve this dessert at special occasions as it is a little too high in sugar and fat to be a daily dessert.

½ cup (3½ oz) black glutinous rice

¼ cup (2 oz) white glutinous rice

1 pandan leaf, tied in a knot

1 vanilla bean, split lengthwise

pinch sea salt

½ cup (4 fl oz) light coconut cream

60 g (2 oz) grated palm sugar (jaggery)

extra light coconut cream, to serve

Soak both the black and white rice in 3 cups (24 fl oz) water for 8 hours. Pour mixture into a medium saucepan and add pandan leaf, vanilla bean and salt. Bring to the boil over medium-high heat. Reduce heat to low and cook, uncovered, stirring often, for 45 minutes or until rice is tender and mixture is thick. Stir in coconut cream and palm sugar. Remove from heat.

Serve warm or at room temperature drizzled with a little extra coconut cream.

SERVES 6

Dessert will keep for 3 days in an airtight container in refrigerator. Reheat before serving, if desired.

roasted stone fruit with toasted almonds & almond cream

Almond cream can be used as a substitute for thick cream or yoghurt. It's very versatile and you can vary the flavour of the yoghurt to suit the dish you are serving it with. Roasted stone fruit make an ideal dessert, but are also delicious for breakfast or brunch, served on their own or with cereal.

1 cinnamon stick

1 vanilla bean, split lengthwise

1 tbsp pure maple syrup

3 peaches

3 nectarines

1/4 cup (1 1/4 oz) toasted flaked almonds

ALMOND CREAM

200 g (6 1/2 oz) vanilla soy yoghurt

50 g (1 3/4 oz) almond meal

2 tsp pure maple syrup, or to taste

To make Almond Cream, combine all ingredients in a bowl and whisk until smooth. If necessary, whisk in a little water to give the consistency of thick cream.

Combine 1 cup (8 fl oz) water, cinnamon stick and vanilla bean in a saucepan and bring to the boil. Reduce heat and simmer until reduced by half. Remove and reserve cinnamon stick and vanilla bean and stir in maple syrup.

Halve stone fruit and place, cut-side up, in a roasting pan with reserved cinnamon stick and vanilla bean. Brush fruit with syrup and roast at 180°C (350°F) for 30 minutes or until fruit is soft, then place under a hot grill (broiler) for 2–3 minutes until fruit is browned on edges. Remove from oven and cool slightly.

Drizzle any juices from the pan over fruit and sprinkle with toasted almonds. Serve with almond cream.

SERVES 4

Almond cream can be prepared a day ahead. Roasted stone fruit can be prepared 3 hours ahead.

GLUTEN-FREE ✔ DAIRY-FREE ✔ DETOX-FRIENDLY ✔

rhubarb & strawberry soufflés

This is a lovely light dessert that is very simple to make. You can measure all the ingredients beforehand so you can make the soufflés quickly, just before serving.

130 g (4$^{1}/_{2}$ oz) rhubarb, cut into
  2 cm ($^{3}/_{4}$ in) lengths

1 tbsp caster (superfine) sugar,
  plus extra to dust

125 g (4 oz) strawberries,
  hulled, quartered

macadamia or grapeseed oil, to grease

3 eggs, separated

$^{1}/_{3}$ cup (2$^{1}/_{2}$ oz) caster (superfine)
  sugar, extra

1 cup (8 fl oz) light soy milk or rice milk

140 g (4$^{1}/_{2}$ oz) container apple puree

1 tbsp macadamia oil

$^{1}/_{3}$ cup (1$^{3}/_{4}$ oz) gluten-free all-purpose
  flour pre-mix

1 egg white, extra

pure icing (confectioners') sugar, to dust

Place rhubarb, sugar and 1 tablespoon water in a saucepan. Bring to a simmer, cover and cook over low heat for 2 minutes or until tender. Stir in strawberries, remove from heat, cover and set aside for 10 minutes.

Brush six 1 cup (8 fl oz) soufflé dishes with oil to lightly grease. Dust inside surface of dishes lightly with caster sugar. Place on an oven tray. Spoon rhubarb mixture evenly into prepared dishes.

Whisk egg yolks and 3 tablespoons of the extra sugar in a bowl until pale and slightly thickened. Whisk in milk, apple puree and oil. Sift the flour over the top and whisk until smooth.

Use an electric beater to whisk all the egg whites in a clean bowl until soft peaks form. Add remaining sugar and whisk until dissolved. Add a large spoon of egg white mixture to the milk mixture and fold in gently. Add remaining whites and fold in until just combined. Spoon mixture into dishes. Bake at 180°C (350°F) for 20 minutes or until soufflés are well risen and golden. Remove from oven and quickly dust with icing sugar before serving immediately.

SERVES 6

Rhubarb and strawberry mixture can be made several hours ahead. Make the soufflés just before serving.

GLUTEN-FREE ✔ **DAIRY-FREE** ✔

old-fashioned trifle

This recipe gives you more than just one dessert. The individual components can be used for other desserts. The sponge can be used to make dishes such as tiramisu (if you tolerate dairy food), the jelly can be poured into individual dishes and served with berries as a light refreshing dessert, and the custard can be served with puddings, such as Steamed Sago Plum Pudding (page 140). You can use vanilla bean infused verjuice syrup in place of wine or grape juice if you like.

½ cup (4 fl oz) sweet white wine
  or grape juice
100 g (3¼ oz) raspberries
125 g (4 oz) strawberries, sliced
1 qty Cinnamon Custard (page 177)
ground cinnamon, to serve
extra raspberries and strawberries

SPONGE CAKE
macadamia or grapeseed oil,
  to grease
2 eggs, separated
⅓ cup (2½ oz) caster
  (superfine) sugar
⅔ cup (3½ oz) gluten-free
  all-purpose flour pre-mix
1½ tsp gluten-free baking powder
2 tbsp light soy milk or rice milk
3 tsp grapeseed oil

BERRY JELLY
100 g (3¼ oz) raspberries
125 g (4 oz) strawberries, hulled
¼ cup (1½ oz) pure icing sugar
3½ tsp powdered gelatine
1¼ cups (10 fl oz) unsweetened
  100% apple and blackcurrant juice

To make Sponge Cake, brush a shallow round 19 cm (7½ in) (base measurement) cake pan with oil to lightly grease. Line the base with baking paper.

Use an electric beater to whisk egg whites in a clean bowl until soft peaks form. Gradually add sugar and whisk for 1 minute or until thick and glossy. Add egg yolks and whisk until just combined.

Sift flour and baking powder over egg mixture. Pour milk and oil down inside of bowl and use a large metal spoon to fold until just combined.

Spoon mixture into prepared pan and bake at 180°C (350°F) for 15 minutes or until cooked when tested with a skewer. Turn onto a wire rack and cool.

To make Berry Jelly, process half the raspberries and half the strawberries with the icing sugar in a food processor or with a hand-held blender until smooth. Sprinkle gelatine over ½ cup (4 fl oz) boiling water in a small jug and whisk with a fork until completely dissolved. Combine berry puree, gelatine mixture and apple and blackcurrant juice in a jug or bowl and mix well.

Cut about three-quarters of the sponge into 2.5 cm (1 in) cubes and place in an 8-cup (64 fl oz) serving bowl. Drizzle wine or grape juice over all the sponge cubes. Scatter raspberries and sliced strawberries over the sponge and gently pour jelly mixture over the top. Cover and refrigerate for 3 hours or until set.

Spoon custard over top of trifle and sprinkle with ground cinnamon.
Serve with extra berries.

SERVES 8

Trifle can be made up to 2 days ahead. Photograph appears on back cover.

steamed sago plum pudding

Serve this pudding with Cinnamon Custard (page 177) if you like. It is beautifully moist and reheats very well.

macadamia oil, to grease

1 1/2 cups (12 fl oz) soy milk
or rice milk

2/3 cup lightly packed
(4 1/2 oz) brown sugar

1/3 cup (2 1/4 oz) sago

2 tbsp macadamia oil

1 1/2 tbsp brandy or rum

1 tsp vanilla extract

1 1/2 tsp mixed spice

1 tsp bicarbonate of soda
(baking soda)

1 tbsp soy milk or rice milk, extra

3 cups lightly packed (9 oz)
fresh gluten-free breadcrumbs

375 g (12 oz) packet mixed
dried fruit

2 eggs, lightly beaten

Brush 8-cup (64 fl oz) pudding basin with oil to lightly grease. Bring the milk to the boil in a saucepan. Remove from heat. Whisk in sugar, sago, oil, brandy or rum, vanilla and mixed spice. Cover and set aside for 30 minutes.

Combine bicarbonate of soda and extra milk in a cup and mix well. Stir into sago mixture.

Combine breadcrumbs and dried fruit in a bowl. Add sago mixture and eggs and mix well. Spoon mixture into pudding basin.

Cut a piece of baking paper and foil large enough to cover basin top and overhang the edge by at least 8 cm (3 1/4 in). Place foil and paper together and make a pleat in the centre. Place over basin top, foil-side up, and tie firmly with string. Trim excess paper and foil to 5 cm (2 in).

Place an upturned saucer in the base of a large saucepan, quarter-fill with boiling water and bring to the boil over high heat. Put pudding basin into the pan, making sure the water comes two-thirds up the side of the basin (add extra boiling water if needed). Cover and boil over medium-high heat, replenishing the boiling water as needed, for 4 hours or until a skewer inserted in the centre of the pudding comes out clean.

Remove paper and foil and turn onto a serving plate. Cut into wedges and serve hot.

SERVES 8–10

The pudding can be made 1 week ahead. Cover pudding in basin with plastic wrap and keep refrigerated. To reheat, steam in the basin for 30 minutes, as outlined in the recipe. Pudding can be removed from basin, wrapped in plastic wrap and frozen in a sealed freezer bag for up to 2 months. Thaw in refrigerator and return to basin before reheating, as outlined above.

GLUTEN-FREE ✓ **DAIRY-FREE** ✓ **LUNCH BOX** ✓

lemon & lime delicious

This is a delicious and simple moist pudding made with lemons with limes. You can use all lemons or all limes if you prefer, or substitute both with orange rind and juice. As a variation, cook the dessert in six individual 1-cup (8 fl oz) ovenproof dishes (they will take 15 minutes at 180°C/350°F).

macadamia oil, to grease

3 eggs, separated

1/3 cup (2 1/2 oz) caster (superfine) sugar

1 cup (8 fl oz) light soy milk or rice milk

2 tbsp macadamia oil

2 tbsp lemon juice

1 tsp finely grated lemon rind

2 tbsp lime juice

1 tsp finely grated lime rind

1/2 cup (2 1/2 oz) gluten-free all-purpose flour pre-mix

1 tsp gluten-free baking powder

Brush a shallow 6 cup (48 fl oz) ovenproof dish with oil to lightly grease.

Whisk egg yolks and 1/4 cup of the sugar in a bowl until pale and slightly thick. Whisk in milk, oil and rind and juice of lemon and lime. Sift flour and baking powder over top and whisk until smooth.

Use an electric beater to whisk egg whites in a clean bowl until soft peaks form. Gradually whisk in remaining sugar. Use a large metal spoon to fold a spoonful of egg whites into the lime mixture until combined. Fold in remaining egg white until just combined. Spoon or pour the mixture into prepared dish.

Bake at 180°C (350°F) for 45 minutes or until set and lightly browned on top (they will remain moist and sticky below top layer).

SERVES 6

Make dessert close to serving time.

baking

JAN: *I confess that I'm the sweet tooth and I find it hard to resist freshly made cakes, biscuits or bread. I am so pleased that we can offer you some lovely gluten-free versions of traditional favourites. The biscotti make a lovely gift if you like baking food for friends. Gavin particularly loves the Yeast-free Hi-fibre Bread (page 146), claiming it's the best gluten-free bread he has tried. He likes it for breakfast with our Hummus (page 177) or with the nut and seed spread that is in our Detox Cookbook (I always keep a batch in the fridge for him). When I'm writing my articles and books, I like a mid-morning munch on our Savoury Biscuits (page 149), eaten either plain or with hummus because they are excellent brain food!*

KATHY: *If we are into confessions, then I must confess that Jan has written all the recipes in this chapter. As she has said, it is a difficult area to work in and I have neither the patience, nor the sweet tooth that would make me persevere. However, I can assure you that these inspiring recipes have been tested time and time again to make sure they are the best we (she) could achieve and I know that like me, you will be delighted with the results. Thanks Jan, I owe you one!*

One difficult area of gluten-free cooking is producing lovely baked breads, cakes and pastry that are as good as those that contain gluten. We have paid particular attention to creating some exceptional recipes for you in this section. A great bonus with gluten-free baking is that you can toss the usual baking rules out the window, such as 'don't overbeat the mixture' and 'don't overwork the pastry or dough' or 'don't re-roll and cut the pastry or dough scraps'. It makes it a very relaxed baking experience because there isn't the gluten to overwork or toughen. As all ovens are slightly different in the temperature they register, you may need to bake your recipes for slightly less or more time. We suggest you put the timer on for 5 minutes less and check the food from that point on to be on the safe side. The oven we used for testing the recipes has a top and bottom element but is not fan-forced. If you have a fan-forced oven, adjust the temperature accordingly.

fried onion, herb & hummus tarts

Crisp fried onion flakes, sold in small jars from Asian grocery stores, add a lovely depth of flavour to these tarts. Serve them piping hot from the oven, or at room temperature, or pack them with a salad as a picnic lunch. To save time, buy ready-made low-fat hummus if you like.

2 cups (10 oz) gluten-free all-purpose
   flour pre-mix
1/2 tsp chilli powder
1/4 tsp gluten-free baking powder
1/4 cup (2 fl oz) extra virgin olive oil
ground paprika

FILLING

6 eggs
1 1/2 cup (12 fl oz) soy milk
3/4 cup (6 1/2 oz) Hummus (page 177)
1/4 cup chopped fresh flat-leaf (Italian)
   parsley
1/4 cup (3/4 oz) ready-made fried onion
1 tsp finely chopped fresh rosemary
olive oil to grease

Sift flour, chilli powder and baking powder into a bowl. Season well with salt and pepper. Make a well in the centre. Add 2/3 cup (5 fl oz) water and the oil and use a round-bladed knife to mix ingredients together, using a cutting motion, until clumps form. Use your hands to finish combining the mixture, then bring mixture together into a firm dough. Knead in a bowl until smooth. Divide dough evenly into 6 portions. Cover and set aside for 20 minutes to rest.

To make filling, whisk eggs, soy milk and hummus together in a jug until well combined. Stir in parsley, onion and rosemary. Season well with salt and pepper.

Brush six 11.5 cm (4 1/4 in) mini pie tins with oil to lightly grease.

Knead a portion of dough until pliable. Roll out between 2 sheets of baking paper to a 16 cm (6 1/4 in) diameter disc. Carefully lift into a greased pie tin, easing pastry into base and side of tin and pressing gently to line the side (pastry may crack on the edges, if so, overlap slightly and press evenly). Repeat rolling and lining tins with remaining portions. Place tins on a large oven tray.

Lightly whisk the filling again and pour evenly into pastry shells. Sprinkle with paprika. Bake at 200°C (400°F) for 20 minutes or until pastry is golden and filling is set in the centre. Set aside for 5 minutes, then carefully slide the tarts from tins onto serving plates.

MAKES 6

GLUTEN-FREE ✔ **DAIRY-FREE** ✔ **DETOX-FRIENDLY** ✔ **LUNCH BOX** ✔

coriander & chilli corn bread

Serve this bread with soups, casseroles or as snack. If you like more chilli heat, increase the ground chillies to 1 teaspoon.

olive oil

1 small brown onion, finely chopped

1 1/2 cups (7 oz) gluten-free self-raising flour

1/4 cup (1 1/4 oz) gluten-free gluten substitute

2 tsp gluten-free baking powder

2 tsp ground coriander (cilantro)

1/2 tsp ground chillies

1/2 tsp ground paprika

1/2 tsp salt

3/4 cup (4 1/2 oz) polenta (yellow cornmeal)

1 tbsp caster (superfine) sugar

2 eggs

1/3 cup (2 1/2 fl oz) olive oil

1 1/2 cups (12 fl oz) soy or rice milk

1/3 cup chopped fresh coriander (cilantro)

2 large fresh red chillies, seeded and finely chopped

Brush a 7 cm (2³/₄ in) deep, 11 x 21 cm (4¹/₄ x 8¹/₄ in) loaf pan with oil to lightly grease. Line the base and 2 long sides with a piece of baking paper.

Heat 1 tbsp olive oil in a small saucepan over medium heat. Add onion and cook, stirring occasionally for 5 minutes or until soft. Set aside to cool for 10 minutes.

Sift flour, gluten substitute, baking powder, ground coriander, ground chillies, paprika and salt into a large bowl. Stir in polenta and sugar and make a well in the centre.

Whisk together eggs, oil and milk and add to dry ingredients. Mix with a wooden spoon until combined. Stir in onion, chopped coriander and fresh chillies.

Spoon batter into lined pan and bake at 180°C (350°F) for 45 minutes or until well browned and cooked when tested with a skewer (the skewer may be a little sticky). Cool in pan for 10 minutes before turning onto a wire rack to cool. Serve warm or at room temperature. Use a serrated knife to cut into slices.

MAKES 1 LOAF

Corn bread will keep in an airtight container in refrigerator for up to 4 days. It can be toasted after 2 days, if desired.

yeast-free hi-fibre bread

Gluten-free bread cannot have the texture of regular bread because gluten gives bread its typical strong, bouncy texture. Gluten-free bread tends to be on the 'cakey' side because of this. Using a gluten substitute helps provide a better texture, as this bread will show. It is delicious served on the day of baking, or up to the next day, but after that, you might prefer to toast it. A word of warning – it's not a very low-fat bread due to the seeds and oil.

olive oil, to grease

2/3 cup (4 oz) potato flour

2/3 cup (3¾ oz) white rice flour

2/3 cup (3 oz) cornflour (cornstarch)

2/3 cup (2½ oz) soy flour

1/3 cup (1½ oz) gluten-free gluten
  substitute

1½ tbsp gluten-free baking powder

½ tsp salt

1/3 cup (2 oz) polenta (yellow cornmeal)

2 tbsp linseeds (flax seeds)

2 tbsp coarsely ground sunflower seeds

2 tbsp sesame seeds

1 egg

1 egg white

1/3 cup (2½ fl oz) olive oil

Brush a 10 cm (4 in) deep, 9 x 22.5 cm (3½ x 9 in) loaf pan with oil to lightly grease. Line the base and 2 long sides with a piece of baking paper.

Sift potato flour, rice flour, cornflour, soy flour, gluten substitute, baking powder and salt into a large bowl. Stir in polenta, linseeds, sunflower seeds and sesame seeds and make a well in the centre.

Whisk together egg, egg white and oil. Gradually stir egg mixture and 2 cups (16 fl oz) water into the dry ingredients to make a soft batter. Pour batter into greased pan and bake at 180°C (350°F) for 55–60 minutes or until risen, golden and cooked when tested with a skewer (the skewer may be slightly sticky). Set aside to cool in the pan for 30 minutes, then transfer to a wire rack to cool completely.

MAKES 1 LOAF

Bread will keep in an airtight container in refrigerator for 4 days.

GLUTEN-FREE ✔   DAIRY-FREE ✔   DETOX-FRIENDLY ✔   LUNCH BOX ✔

olive & thyme focaccia

The texture of this focaccia is such that you can make a sandwich by splitting a portion and filling it. It is also fabulous served with dips and antipasto. Use self-raising flour and omit the yeast if you are on a yeast-free diet.

olive oil, to grease

2⅔ cups (13 oz) gluten-free all-purpose flour

¼ cup (1¼ oz) gluten substitute

7 g (2 tsp/1 sachet) dried yeast

¼ tsp salt

¼ tsp sugar

12 kalamata olives, pitted, chopped

2 tsp fresh thyme leaves

2 small fresh red chillies, seeded, finely chopped

1 egg, lightly whisked

1 tbsp extra virgin olive oil

1½ tsp fennel seeds

1 tsp sea salt

Brush a 20 x 30 cm (8 x 12 in) lamington pan with oil to lightly grease.

Sift flour, gluten substitute, yeast, salt and sugar into a large bowl. Add the olives, thyme, chillies and season with pepper. Make a well in the centre.

Add 1¾ cups (14 fl oz) warm water and egg and mix well to make a batter. Spread batter over base of greased pan. Use a lightly wet hand to finish patting mixture over base of pan. Drizzle with the oil, then tilt pan to spread oil evenly. Sprinkle with fennel seeds and sea salt. Cover pan with plastic wrap and a cloth. Set aside in a warm place for 30 minutes to rise.

Remove plastic wrap and bake at 220°C (425°F) for 40 minutes, then cover loosely with a piece of foil and bake for a further 10 minutes or until well browned (a skewer inserted may come out sticky). Transfer to a wire rack to cool. Cut as desired to serve.

SERVES 6–8

Focaccia is best eaten on day of making, however, it will toast well for up to 2 days afterwards.

GLUTEN-FREE ✔ DAIRY-FREE ✔

savoury biscuits

These biscuits are ideal to serve with toppings as canapés. They also team nicely with dips and are very more-ish on their own. They are not terribly low in fat so it is best not to overindulge in one sitting.

1 cup (3 1/2 oz) quinoa flakes

3/4 cup (2 3/4 oz) rolled brown rice flakes

1 cup (5 oz) gluten-free all-purpose flour
  pre-mix

1 tbsp brown sugar

1/2 tsp baking powder

1/2 tsp salt

1/2 cup (4 fl oz) olive, macadamia or
  grapeseed oil

Place quinoa, rice flakes, flour, sugar, baking powder and salt in a food processor and process until rice flakes are finely chopped. Add oil and 1/2 cup (4 fl oz) water and process until mixture forms moist clumps. Transfer to a bowl and use your hands to bring mixture together into a firm dough (add an extra tablespoon of water if needed) and knead lightly. Divide dough into four portions.

Knead a portion of dough in your hands until pliable, then roll between 2 sheets of baking paper until 3 mm (1/8 in) thick. Use a 5.5 cm (2 1/4 in) diameter round cutter to cut discs from the dough. Carefully peel discs from the paper and place on two large oven trays lined with baking paper. Re-roll the dough scraps and cut out more discs. Repeat with remaining dough portions. Bake batches in oven at 200°C (400°F) for 10 minutes, swapping trays halfway, or until biscuits are golden on the edges and bubbling (they will appear a little oily). Cool on trays (biscuits will brown a little more on cooling).

MAKES ABOUT 70

Biscuits will keep in an airtight container for 2 weeks.

GLUTEN-FREE ✓ **DAIRY-FREE** ✓

apple & marmalade tea cake

This cake is for special occasions and is not that suitable as a daily treat because it is quite high in sugar and fat. It is a wonderful cake for people with wheat, gluten or dairy intolerance or allergy. This tea cake is especially good served warm with warm custard – dairy-free of course.

⅔ cup (5 fl oz) macadamia or grapeseed oil, plus extra to grease

½ cup (3½ oz) raw sugar

3 large eggs

2 tbsp 100% spreadable fruit orange marmalade

1 cup (5 oz) gluten-free self-raising flour

½ cup (2 oz) gluten-free all-purpose flour

2 tbsp gluten-free gluten substitute

2 tbsp soy or rice milk

3 large Granny Smith apples, peeled, quartered, cored

2 tbsp 100% spreadable fruit orange marmalade, extra

Brush a 20 cm (8 in) springform pan (base facing flat-side up) with oil to lightly grease. Line base with non-stick baking paper.

Whisk together oil, sugar, eggs and marmalade in a bowl. Sift flours and gluten substitute over top and stir in with the milk using a wooden spoon. Beat well to make a smooth batter. Spread batter evenly into prepared pan.

Score the rounded side of the apple quarters (you will need 9 quarters) lengthwise and deeply, without cutting right through, at 3 mm (1/8 in) intervals. Arrange the apple quarters, scored-side up, around the outside edge and in the centre of the cake batter. Bake at 180°C (350°F) for 55–60 minutes or until cake is cooked when tested with a skewer.

Meanwhile, combine extra marmalade and 1 tablespoon water in a small saucepan. Stir over low heat until combined. Brush mixture over hot cake when it comes out of the oven. Cool a little in the pan then turn onto a wire rack. Serve warm or at room temperature.

SERVES 8

Cake best served on day of baking.

GLUTEN-FREE ✔ **DAIRY-FREE** ✔

banana, carrot & walnut cake

This is a lovely moist cake that goes down a treat. You can ice it if you like but remember that icing adds extra sugar and fat to the waistline (we would rather save those kilojoules for the occasional glass of good wine!).

macadamia or grapeseed oil, to grease

1/2 cup (4 1/2 oz) mashed ripe banana

1/2 cup (3 1/2 oz) finely grated carrot

1/2 cup (3 1/2 oz) raw sugar

1/2 cup (2 oz) chopped walnuts

1/3 cup (2 1/2 fl oz) soy or rice milk

1/3 cup (2 1/2 fl oz) macadamia or
   grapeseed oil

2 eggs

1 1/2 cups (7 oz) gluten-free self-raising
   flour

2 tbsp gluten-free gluten substitute

1 tsp mixed spice

Brush a 6.5 cm (2 1/2 in) deep, 9.5 x 19.5 cm (3 3/4 x 7 1/2 in) (base measurement) loaf pan with oil to lightly grease. Line the base and 2 long sides with non-stick baking paper.

Place banana, carrot, sugar, walnuts, milk, oil and eggs in a large mixing bowl. Use a wooden spoon to mix until well combined. Sift flour, gluten substitute and mixed spice over the top and use a wooden spoon to mix until well combined.

Pour mixture into prepared pan, smooth the surface and bake at 180°C (350°F) for 55–60 minutes or until cooked when tested with a skewer (the skewer may be slightly sticky). Set aside to cool in pan for 10 minutes, then turn onto a wire rack to cool to room temperature.

MAKES 1 LOAF

Cake will keep for 4 days in an airtight container.

GLUTEN-FREE ✔ **DAIRY-FREE** ✔

rich fruit cake

This is a dense full-flavoured fruit cake – a thin slice is all you need. We used preservative-free dried cherries in preference to glacé cherries, which are full of food colourings and preservatives.

375 g (12 oz) sultanas

250 g (8 oz) raisins, large ones halved

250 g (8 oz) pitted dates, chopped

250 g (8 oz) currants

240 g (7 3/4 oz) dried cherries, large ones halved

125 g (4 oz) dried figs, chopped

1/2 cup (4 fl oz) brandy or rum

2/3 cup lightly packed (4 1/2 oz) brown sugar

180ml (6 fl oz) macadamia or grapeseed oil

5 eggs

1 cup (5 oz) gluten-free self-raising flour

1 cup (5 oz) gluten-free all-purpose flour pre-mix

1/2 tsp xanthan gum

2 tsp mixed spice

1 tsp ground cinnamon

2 tbsp brandy or rum, extra

Place dried fruit into a glass or ceramic bowl and pour brandy or rum over the top. Mix well. Cover and set aside overnight to macerate, stirring occasionally.

Line base and side of a deep, round 22 cm (8 1/2 in) cake pan with 2 layers of non-stick baking paper.

Whisk sugar, apple puree, oil and eggs together in a large mixing bowl. Add dried fruit mixture and mix well. Sift flours, xanthan gum, mixed spice and cinnamon over the top and mix gently until well combined. Spoon mixture into prepared pan and spread evenly. Tap pan several times on bench to settle the mixture. Smooth the surface.

Bake at 150°C (300°F) on the lowest shelf for 2 1/2–2 3/4 hours (covering with a piece of foil after 1 1/2 hours to prevent overbrowning) or until a skewer inserted into the centre comes out clean. Pour extra brandy or rum over the hot cake.

Wrap cake in its pan in several clean tea towels and set aside to cool to room temperature. Remove cake from the pan and remove paper. Wrap in plastic wrap and store in an airtight container. Cut into thin slices to serve.

MAKES 1 CAKE

This cake can be stored in an airtight container for up to 2 months. It can also be wrapped in plastic wrap and placed in a sealed freezer bag in the freezer for up to 6 months. Thaw in the refrigerator.

pistachio, fig & orange biscotti

These biscotti are lovely to serve after dinner or for afternoon tea with a good cup of tea (herbal of course).

macadamia or vegetable oil, to grease

1 cup (5 oz) gluten-free all-purpose flour pre-mix

1/2 cup (2 3/4 oz) finely chopped dried figs

1/2 cup (2 3/4 oz) pistachio kernels

3 egg whites

1/3 cup (2 1/2 oz) caster (superfine) sugar

1 1/2 tbsp finely grated orange rind

Brush an 8 x 17.5 cm (3 1/4 x 6 1/2 in) (base measurement) loaf pan with oil to lightly grease. Line the base and 2 wide sides with a strip of non-stick baking paper, allowing it to overhang the sides.

Combine flour and figs in a small bowl and use your fingers to separate the fig pieces and coat them with flour. Place pistachio kernels in a small heatproof bowl and cover with boiling water. Set aside for 5 minutes to soak until skins soften. Drain. Peel off skins and dry on paper towel.

Meanwhile, use an electric beater to whisk egg whites in a clean, dry bowl until soft peaks form. Add sugar, a spoonful at a time, whisking well after each addition, until sugar dissolves. Add orange rind and whisk until just combined.

Use a large metal spoon to fold the fig mixture and pistachios into the egg white mixture until just combined. Spoon mixture into lined pan and smooth the surface. Bake at 180°C (350°F) for 30 minutes or until firm and cooked through. Remove from pan and cool on a wire rack for 1 hour.

Use a serrated or electric knife to thinly trim the narrow ends from the loaf. Use the knife to cut the loaf crosswise into 5 mm (1/4 in) thick slices. Place slices in a single layer on a large baking tray. Bake in a 120°C (235°F) oven for 30 minutes or until dry, crisp and light golden. Cool on the tray.

MAKES ABOUT 24

Biscotti will keep in an airtight container for up to 1 month.

small bites

JAN: I never put out cheese platters or creamy dips for pre-dinner nibbles when entertaining, as these foods are overly filling and high in unhealthy saturated fat. I usually serve foods like the Vegetable Frittata Bites (page 163). The Fig & Date Nutty Slice (page 164) is a very good sweet treat because it keeps for weeks and you can cut a thin slice as you like to satisfy even the worst sugar craving. I think you will enjoy these recipes, particularly if you get frustrated at parties if most of the finger foods are made from wheat and dairy products.

For drinks, I make a point of drinking lots of water during the day and usually have a cup of oolong tea with breakfast. The Green Chai Tea (page 170) reminds me of a trip I took to India some years ago and I've been hooked on it ever since.

KATHY: I am not much of a snacker; I am more of a three-meals-a-day girl. However, I do love a little treat in the evening while I am preparing dinner. If I am detoxing I might have a glass of juice and a handful of our Indian Spiced Nut & Seed Mix (page 158), or if we're entertaining, I find that the Vegetarian Rice Paper Rolls (page 162) double as a snack/entree and are a good casual way to start a meal.

I drink at least 2 litres (64 fl oz) of water a day, plus several cups of herbal tea, usually mint. Occasionally I treat myself to a decaffeinated coffee because I love the taste, but I steer clear of the real thing as I know that caffeine will always have an adverse effect on me. I love fresh juices and always leave my juicer machine on the kitchen bench ready to spring into action.

Most of our 'small bites' recipes are only intended for when you are entertaining, not necessarily to snack on every day, unless we mention otherwise. One problem we have in Western countries is that we snack too much on high-kilojoule foods between meals, which is a major contributor to people being overweight (see 10 ways to reduce and manage your weight, pages 10–13). For snacks, both of us might have a small handful of nuts most days or we recommend you snack on fresh fruit, vegetable sticks or soy yoghurt.

Top of the list when talking about drinks should be water, but you don't need a recipe for that, just a reminder to drink about 1.5 litres (48 fl oz) to keep hydrated every day so you look and feel your best. After that, we have given you a selection of hot and cold drinks to serve to guests or to enjoy every day.

indian spiced nut & seed mix

These are a fabulous nibbly food to put out for guests at your next dinner party and they make a wonderful snack to take to work – but beware, they are very addictive! As nuts contain 50 to 70 per cent fat (albeit very good fat), you do need to eat them in moderation or you could expand your waistline.

1 cup (4$\frac{1}{2}$ oz) unsalted macadamia nuts

1 cup (4$\frac{3}{4}$ oz) unsalted cashews

1 cup (4$\frac{3}{4}$ oz) brazil nuts

$\frac{1}{3}$ cup (1$\frac{3}{4}$ oz) pinenuts

$\frac{1}{3}$ cup (1$\frac{3}{4}$ oz) pepitas (pumpkin seeds)

2 tsp grapeseed oil

1 tbsp panch pora

1$\frac{1}{2}$ tsp garam masala

$\frac{1}{2}$–1 tsp chilli powder

2 tsp wheat-free tamari sauce

1 tbsp caster (superfine) sugar

Combine macadamias, cashews and brazil nuts and spread on an oven tray. Bake at 200°C (400°F) for 8 minutes. Toss the nuts on the tray, then add pinenuts and pepitas. Cook for a further 4–5 minutes or until nuts are toasted.

Meanwhile, heat oil in a small saucepan over medium heat. Add panch pora and cook, stirring, for 30 seconds or until mustard seeds begin to pop. Remove from heat and stir in garam masala and chilli powder. Transfer mixture to a large heatproof bowl and stir in tamari and sugar.

Add hot nuts and seeds to the bowl and toss continuously to coat in the spiced mixture until the moisture has evaporated.

Spread nut and seed mixture over the baking tray and return to the oven for 1 minute. Cool on the tray (the coating will become crisp on cooling). Transfer cold nuts to an airtight container.

MAKES ABOUT 3²/₃ CUPS

Nuts will become sticky if left uncovered, so keep in an airtight container until ready to serve. Nuts will keep in the container in a cool cupboard for up to 6 weeks.

GLUTEN-FREE ✔   DAIRY-FREE ✔   DETOX-FRIENDLY ✔

moroccan spiced beef patties with tomato salsa

Serve the patties as finger food when entertaining, pack them in the kids' lunch boxes or take on picnics. They are also delicious made with minced lamb or chicken.

olive oil

1 medium onion, finely chopped

1 large garlic clove, finely chopped

1 tsp ground coriander

1/2 tsp ground cumin

1/2 tsp ground turmeric

1/2 tsp paprika

400 g (13 oz) lean minced (ground) beef

1/2 cup (2 oz) gluten-free breadcrumbs made from day-old bread

2 tbsp soy milk

2 tbsp chopped fresh flat-leaf (Italian) parsley

2 tbsp chopped fresh coriander (cilantro)

1 egg, lightly whisked

TOMATO SALSA

3 tsp olive oil

1 small onion, finely chopped

1 clove garlic, crushed

1 tsp ground coriander

400 g (13 oz) can diced tomatoes in juice

2 tbsp chopped fresh coriander (cilantro)

1 tsp finely grated lemon rind

To make Tomato Salsa, heat oil in a saucepan over medium heat. Add onion and cook, stirring occasionally, for 5 minutes or until soft. Add garlic and ground coriander and cook for 1 minute. Stir in tomatoes and bring to the boil. Reduce heat to low and cook, stirring occasionally, for 20–25 minutes or until thick. Remove from heat and stir in chopped coriander and lemon rind. Season with salt and pepper. Set aside to cool.

To make patties, heat 1 tablespoon oil in a small saucepan over medium heat. Add onion and cook over low heat, stirring occasionally, for 5 minutes or until soft. Add garlic, ground coriander, cumin, turmeric and paprika and cook, stirring, for 30 seconds or until fragrant. Transfer to a bowl and set aside to cool for 10 minutes. Add beef, breadcrumbs, milk, parsley, chopped coriander and egg. Season well with salt and pepper. Mix thoroughly.

Shape 1 tablespoon of beef mixture into a ball and place on a tray. Repeat with remaining mixture.

Heat 1 tablespoon olive oil in a large frying pan over medium heat. Add half the meatballs and flatten slightly into patties. Cook for 3 minutes or until browned underneath. Gently turn patties and cook for 3 minutes or until browned underneath and just cooked through. Line an oven tray with paper towel and place patties on tray in the oven at 100°C (200°F) to keep warm. Cook remaining patties.

To serve, place patties on a serving platter and top each with a dollop of Tomato Salsa.

MAKES ABOUT 24

pumpkin & pepita pizza bites

You can also cut the pizza into larger serves to have as a light meal with a crisp salad if you like. Served like this it would serve 4.

olive oil, to grease

350 g (12 oz) firm pumpkin (squash),
  seeded, peeled, cut into 1.5 cm
  (⁵/₈ in) cubes

1/3 cup (1³/₄ oz) kalamata olives,
  pitted, quartered

2 tbsp pepitas (pumpkin seeds)

2 tsp extra virgin olive oil

1 tsp fresh thyme leaves

1 small fresh red chilli, seeded,
  thinly sliced

1³/₄ cups (8¹/₂ oz) gluten-free
  all-purpose flour pre-mix

1 tsp (¹/₂ sachet) dried yeast

¹/₄ tsp salt

¹/₄ tsp sugar

2 tbsp chopped fresh flat-leaf
  (Italian) parsley

1 egg, lightly whisked

3 tsp extra virgin olive oil, extra

TOMATO SAUCE

2 tsp extra virgin olive oil

1 small onion, finely chopped

1 clove garlic, finely chopped

400 g (13 oz) can diced tomatoes
  in juice

1 tsp fresh thyme leaves

To make Tomato Sauce, heat oil in a saucepan over medium heat. Add onion and cook, stirring occasionally, for 5 minutes or until softened. Add garlic and cook for 1 minute. Stir in tomatoes and thyme and cook, uncovered, stirring often, for 20 minutes or until reduced by one third and thickened. Set aside to cool.

Brush a 25 x 31 cm (10 x 12¹/₂ in) Swiss roll pan with oil to lightly grease. Line base with non-stick paper.

Combine pumpkin, olives, pepitas, oil, thyme and chilli in a bowl and toss well. Season with pepper.

Sift flour, yeast, salt and sugar into a bowl. Stir in parsley and make a well in the centre. Add ³/₄ cup (6 fl oz) warm water and the egg and mix to a smooth batter.

Spread mixture evenly over base of prepared pan using a wet spatula (dip the spatula in water occasionally when batter begins to stick). You may need to finish with a wet hand. Spoon Tomato Sauce on top and spread evenly. Scatter pumpkin mixture evenly over tomato sauce.

Drizzle with the extra oil and bake at 220°C (425°F) for 30 minutes or until bubbling on top and golden underneath. Transfer pizza to a cutting board and cut evenly into 36 squares. Serve hot.

SERVES 6 (appetiser)

Pizza is best made close to serving. Tomato sauce can be made up to 2 days ahead.

GLUTEN-FREE ✔   DAIRY-FREE ✔

vegetarian rice paper rolls

Rice paper rolls would have to be one of the healthiest 'fast foods' you can make or buy, as they are very low in fat and full of vegetables. Our rolls can be made a little ahead and packed for lunches, served as finger food or given to the children as a great snack food. For a change, add a little shredded cooked chicken, small peeled prawns or some chopped tofu to the filling mixture instead of the egg.

1 tsp grapeseed oil

2 eggs, lightly whisked

1 x 160 g (5 oz) carrot, cut into julienne

1 x 160 g (5 oz) zucchini (courgette), cut into julienne

50 g (1¾ oz) rice vermicelli noodles

18 x 21 cm (8¼ in) diameter rice paper wrappers

1 large green (spring) onion (scallion), cut into julienne

¼ cup firmly packed fresh mint leaves

¼ cup firmly packed torn fresh basil leaves

¼ cup lightly packed fresh coriander (cilantro) leaves

⅓ cup (2 oz) roasted unsalted peanuts, chopped

DIPPING SAUCE

¼ cup (2 fl oz) fresh lime juice

1½ tbsp fish sauce

1 tbsp sugar

1 small clove garlic, crushed

1 small fresh red chilli, seeded, finely chopped

To make Dipping Sauce, combine lime juice, ¼ cup (2 fl oz) water, fish sauce, sugar, garlic and chilli in a screw-top jar and shake until the sugar dissolves.

Heat oil in a small omelette or frying pan over medium heat. Add eggs and cook over medium-low heat for 3–5 minutes or until just set in the centre. Place omelette on a board and set aside to cool. Halve omelette, then cut crosswise into 1 cm (½ in) wide strips.

Meanwhile, place carrot, zucchini and rice noodles in separate heatproof bowls. Pour enough boiling water into each bowl to cover the ingredients. Cover bowls and set aside for 5 minutes or until vegetables are soft and noodles are tender. Drain and set aside to cool.

Soak a rice paper wrapper in a shallow, wide dish or pan of very hot water for 30 seconds or until translucent. Lift onto a clean tea towel. Place a little of the omelette, carrot, zucchini, noodles, green onion, mint, basil, coriander and peanuts in a neat pile, 5 cm (2 in) in from the closest edge of the rice paper. Fold edge over filling, fold in sides, then roll up firmly, enclosing filling. Place on a tray and cover with a damp clean tea towel.

Repeat with remaining rice paper wrappers and filling ingredients. Cover tray tightly with plastic wrap until ready to serve. Serve rolls at room temperature with Dipping Sauce.

MAKES 18 ROLLS

Rolls can be made up to 3 hours ahead. Keep tightly covered at room temperature if serving within an hour, or in refrigerator until ready to serve. The dipping sauce can be made up to 3 days ahead. The rolls without the sauce are detox-friendly. To pack for lunches, wrap rolls individually in plastic wrap (wrapped like this they keep for up to 1 day).

GLUTEN-FREE ✓ **DAIRY-FREE** ✓ **LUNCH BOX** ✓

vegetable frittata bites

Children love this frittata and toddlers enjoy eating it with their fingers, so this is a great recipe to make for childrens' lunch boxes. Pack some frittata pieces with a salad and some rice or bread. You can halve the recipe and bake in a small square pan if you would prefer to make less.

1 tbsp extra virgin olive oil,
plus extra to grease

1 small brown onion, finely chopped

1 cup firmly packed (5¾ oz)
grated carrot

1 cup firmly packed (3 oz)
grated green zucchini (courgette)

½ cup (2½ oz) finely chopped red
capsicum (pepper)

½ cup firmly packed (3 oz)
grated potato

8 eggs

2½ tbsp gluten-free all-purpose flour

4 large finely chopped green (spring)
onions (scallions)

¼ cup chopped fresh parsley

¼ cup chopped fresh chives

2 tbsp baby capers

1 tsp finely grated lemon rind

Brush a 23 cm (9 in) square slab pan with oil to lightly grease. Line the base and sides with baking paper, allowing paper to overhang the edges.

Heat oil in a frying pan over medium heat. Add onion and cook, stirring occasionally, for 5 minutes or until soft and beginning to brown. Add carrot, zucchini, capsicum and potato and cook, stirring, for 4 minutes or until vegetables are soft. Set aside to cool for 20 minutes.

Whisk eggs in a large bowl. Whisk in flour, taking care to remove lumps. Stir in the vegetable mixture, green onions, parsley, chives, capers and lemon rind. Season well with salt and pepper.

Pour mixture into prepared pan and smooth the surface. Bake at 180°C (350°F) for 25–30 minutes or until set in the centre. Set aside for 20 minutes to cool. Use the paper to lift frittata from pan onto a board. Slice evenly into small rectangles or squares with a sharp knife. Serve warm.

MAKES ABOUT 24 PIECES

Frittata can be made up to 3 hours ahead. Reheat it in a 120°C (235°F) oven for 15 minutes before serving if you like. Leftovers will keep in the refrigerator in an airtight container for up to 2 days.

fig & date nutty slice

This is a very healthy sweet slice full of dietary fibre due to the nuts, coconut and fruit. We like to serve it after dinner with tea or coffee or you could eat it as an afternoon snack. If you like, use other nuts.

⅔ cup (3 oz) hazelnuts

⅔ cup (2 oz) walnut halves

½ cup (1 ½ oz) desiccated
    coconut

125 g (4 oz) dried figs,
    finely chopped

125 g (4 oz) pitted dried dates,
    finely chopped

1 tbsp macadamia oil

⅓ cup (1 ¾ oz) sunflower seeds

Spread hazelnuts and walnuts on separate oven trays. Toast at 180°C (350°F) for 5–7 minutes or until lightly browned and fragrant. Place hazelnuts in a clean tea towel and rub to remove the skins. Cool both nuts and combine. Put half the nuts in a food processor and process until finely ground. Finely chop remaining nuts. Set aside.

Spread coconut on an oven tray and toast at 180°C (350°F) for 4–5 minutes, stirring well every 2 minutes, or until evenly lightly browned and fragrant. Cool.

Place figs, dates, ⅔ cup (5 fl oz) water and the oil in a saucepan. Bring to a simmer over medium-high heat. Reduce heat to low, cover and cook very gently, stirring often to prevent mixture from sticking, for 10 minutes or until thick. Remove lid and cook for a further 2 minutes or until moisture has evaporated.

Stir in ground and chopped hazelnuts, walnuts and sunflower seeds and mix well. Set aside to cool.

Spread half the coconut on a piece of baking paper. Spoon date mixture down centre of coconut in a rough log shape, about 4 cm (1½ in) diameter. Sprinkle remaining coconut over top and firmly shape mixture into a smooth log by using the paper to turn the log. Place in an airtight container in refrigerator overnight. Cut into 1.5 cm (⅝ in) wide slices with a sharp knife, just before serving.

MAKES ABOUT 16 SLICES

The uncut log will keep for up to 3 weeks in an airtight container in refrigerator.

GLUTEN-FREE ✔ **DAIRY-FREE** ✔ **DETOX-FRIENDLY** ✔ **LUNCH BOX** ✔

nut & seed muesli bars

These bars are very more-ish and a great snack to have on hand for children and teens (not to mention adults). Use purchased gluten-free muesli if you prefer. The bars are not low-fat so don't overindulge.

½ cup (4 fl oz) macadamia or
   grapeseed oil, plus extra to grease
⅓ cup (2½ fl oz) honey
3 eggs
4 cups (14 oz) Nut & Seed Muesli
   (page 22)
½ cup (3 oz) sultanas
1 cup (5 oz) gluten-free self-raising flour,
   sifted
1 tsp ground cinnamon

Brush a 21 x 30 cm (8¼ x 12 in) 3-cm deep cake pan with oil to lightly grease. Line base and 2 long sides with a piece of baking paper, allowing ends to overhang.

Whisk together oil, honey and eggs until combined. Place muesli and sultanas in a large bowl. Sift flour and cinnamon over the top. Add egg mixture and mix until well combined. Spread mixture evenly into prepared pan.

Bake at 180°C (350°F) for 20 minutes or until golden. Cool in pan. Lift onto a board and use a sharp serrated knife to cut into bars.

MAKES ABOUT 24 BARS

Bars will keep for up to 2 weeks in an airtight container in refrigerator.

GLUTEN-FREE ✔   DAIRY-FREE ✔   DETOX-FRIENDLY ✔   LUNCH BOX ✔

spring fruit salad
with coconut & palm sugar

This fruit salad makes a fabulous fruit snack to have during the day or a lovely light dessert. Add a handful of mixed seeds and you have a light breakfast. In summer, try mango, pineapple, raspberries and nectarines. A very pretty mix for autumn is fuyu (crisp persimmon), figs, kiwifruit and grapes. And for winter try apple, custard apple, pink grapefruit and star fruit.

1 peach, halved, roughly chopped

6 strawberries, hulled, quartered

4 loquats, halved, peeled

1 small banana, sliced

1 tbsp lime or lemon juice

1 tbsp flaked coconut

3 tsp grated palm sugar (jaggery)

5 fresh mint leaves, shredded

vanilla soy yoghurt

Combine peach, strawberries, loquats and banana in a bowl. Drizzle with juice and add coconut, palm sugar and mint. Toss gently to combine. Serve topped with a dollop of yoghurt.

SERVES 2

Fruit salad will keep for a day in an airtight container in refrigerator.

GLUTEN-FREE ✔ DAIRY-FREE ✔ DETOX-FRIENDLY ✔

asian virgin mary

This is a non-alcoholic version of a Bloody Mary. We enjoy this drink on a summer's day when tomatoes are at their flavoursome best. Use canned tomato juice if tomatoes are not in season.

400 g (13 oz) ripe tomatoes, quartered

1 small carrot, cut into pieces

½ stick celery

½ tsp finely grated lime rind

2 tsp lime juice

1½ tsp wheat-free tamari sauce

½ tsp sambal oelek

¼ tsp grated palm sugar (jaggery) or brown sugar

freshly ground black pepper

ice cubes

2 stems lemongrass, bruised

Process tomatoes, carrot and celery in a juice extractor and pour into a cocktail shaker. Add lime rind and juice, tamari, sambal oelek, sugar, pepper and ice cubes. Cover and shake until well chilled.

Pour into 2 glasses and add lemongrass. Stir well with lemongrass and serve immediately.

SERVES 2

Juice can be extracted several hours ahead. Keep in refrigerator. Make drink just before serving.

moroccan mint tea

If you've experienced Moroccan tea, you'll know that it is highly scented with mint and very sweet. We've kept the uplifting flavour and toned down the sugar somewhat. The best green tea to use in Moroccan mint tea is gunpowder green tea. The tea looks beautiful served in patterned tea glasses.

3 tsp green tea leaves

1/3 cup firmly packed fresh mint leaves

1 1/2 tbsp sugar

extra fresh mint leaves

Place the tea leaves in a large warmed teapot or plunger pot and add 4 cups (32 fl oz) boiling water. Cover and steep for 2 minutes. Stir in mint leaves and sugar, cover and steep for a further 4 minutes.

Place one or two mint leaves in each serving glass. Strain tea into glasses and serve hot.

SERVES 4–6

Tea best made just before serving.

GLUTEN-FREE ✔ **DAIRY-FREE** ✔

green chai tea

If you don't like soy milk, make this recipe using water and serve it as a lighter version. We have used green tea leaves because green tea is full of highly beneficial antioxidants. If you prefer, use black tea leaves.

1 1/2 cups (12 fl oz) soy milk

2 tsp green tea leaves

4 cm (1 1/2 in) cinnamon stick, crumbled

5 green cardamom pods, lightly crushed

5 whole cloves

2 tsp grated fresh ginger

sugar or honey, to sweeten (optional)

Pour milk and 1/2 cup (4 fl oz) water into a saucepan. Add tea, cinnamon, cardamom, cloves and ginger and bring to the boil over medium heat. Remove from heat, cover and set aside for 5 minutes to steep.

Strain into cups, sweeten if desired, and serve hot.

SERVES 2

Tea best made just before serving.

GLUTEN-FREE ✔ **DAIRY-FREE** ✔ **DETOX-FRIENDLY** ✔

watermelon & strawberry smoothie

This smoothie makes the most refreshing warm weather drink you can imagine. We have lightened it with soda water which makes it feel more like a cocktail. This is an ideal drink to serve at cocktail parties as a 'mocktail'.

570 g (1 lb 2 oz) watermelon, chilled, rind removed, seeded and roughly chopped
200 g (6¹/₂ oz) strawberries, chilled and hulled
2 tbsp lime juice
2 tsp grated fresh ginger
2 tsp finely chopped fresh lemongrass
soda water, to serve
ice cubes, to serve

Place watermelon, strawberries, lime juice, ginger and lemongrass in a blender. Blend to a smooth puree.

Two-thirds fill serving glasses with watermelon mixture, top with soda water and ice cubes and serve.

SERVES 2–4

Puree will keep for 1 day in refrigerator. It will also freeze for 2 weeks.

seasonal menus

These menus have been developed so that the food works well over each day and you get a good mix of dishes over the week. You don't have to stick to this, but it will give you some idea of how the dishes work together. It may not be practical to cook the dishes we have suggested for lunch during the week, especially if you are working. Instead, you could take leftovers from dinner, or make one of our salads (see Basic Recipes, page 174) or a soup at the beginning of the week and take that to work. We have suggested desserts for the weekend, when you are likely to have more time, might be entertaining, or simply feel like indulging.

AUTUMN-WINTER MENU

	BREAKFAST	LUNCH	DINNER
Monday	Potato Cakes with Wilted Spinach & Poached Eggs (page 24)	Middle Eastern Lentils & Rice with Cabbage Salad (page 70)	Swordfish Kebabs with Shaved Fennel & Broad bean Salad (page 117)
Tuesday	Apple Breakfast Muffins (page 32)	Marinated Octopus with Parsley & White Bean Salad (page 63)	Sweet Potato Frittata with Walnut & Herb Salsa (page 124)
Wednesday	Nut & Seed Muesli with soy milk (page 22)	Chicken, Leek & Potato Soup with Peas (page 36)	Lamb Backstraps with Mushroom Risotto & Parsley Puree (page 95)
Thursday	Home-style Baked Beans (page 28)	Open Steak Sandwich with Caramelised Onions (page 53)	Sesame Chicken with Rice Noodles & Cashews (page 87)
Friday	Quinoa & Rice Porridge with Linseeds & Dried Vine fruit (page 29)	Warm Pumpkin, Beetroot & Chickpea Salad with Tahini Sauce (page 78)	Herb-crusted Blue Eye with Cauliflower Puree (page 107) Pineapple, Ginger & Lemongrass Granita (page 134)
Saturday	Scrambled Eggs (page 25)	Chicken, Pork & Veal Terrine (page 38)	Osso Bucco with White Bean Mash (page 99) Rhubarb & Berry Soufflés (page 138)
Sunday	Indian-style Eggs with Yeast-free Hi-fibre Bread (page 146)	Chargrilled Sardines with Celeriac Remoulade (page 61)	Indian Spiced Nut & Seed Mix (page 158) Vegetable Biryani with Pumpkin Dahl (page 120) Lemon & Lime Delicious (page 141)

SPRING-SUMMER MENU

	BREAKFAST	LUNCH	DINNER
Monday	French Toast with Fruit Compote (page 31)	Spiced Rare Beef with Roasted Sweet Potato & Split Pea Sauce (page 49)	Marinated Chicken with Saffron Onions & Quinoa (page 84)
Tuesday	Indian-style Eggs (page 26) with Yeast-free Hi-fibre Bread (page 146)	Grilled Kofta with Pomegranate & Parsley Salad (page 52)	Chargrilled Tuna with Eggplant Jam (page 103)
Wednesday	Apple Breakfast Muffins (page 32)	Chicken, Leek & Potato Soup with Peas (page 36)	Pork Vindaloo with Spicy Green Beans (page 102)
Thursday	Creamy Bircher Muesli (page 21)	Marinated Quail with Red Cabbage Salad (page 40)	Moroccan Mint Tea (page 170) Morrocan Lentil Soup (page126) with Baby Spinach & Pomegranate Seed Salad (page 176)
Friday	Nut & Seed Muesli with soy milk (page 22)	Venison Fillets with Moroccan Date Salad (page 47)	Watermelon & Strawberry Smoothie (page 171) Barramundi Baked in Banana Leaves with Cucumber Salad & Coconut Rice (page 113) Roasted Stone Fruit with Toasted Almonds & Almond Cream (page 136)
Saturday	Buckwheat & Blueberry Soufflé Pancakes with Scented Hazelnut Syrup (page 20)	Steamed Cuttlefish & Prawns with Vietnamese-style Coleslaw (page 54)	Vegetable Antipasto (page 72) Greek-style Roast Chicken with Avgolemono Sauce (page 86) Old Fashioned Trifle (page 139)
Sunday	Scrambled Eggs with toasted Yeast-free Hi-fibre Bread (page 25)	Fish Soup with Capsicum & Almond Rouille (page 58)	Baked Pumpkin 'Gnocchi' with Roasted Tomatoes & Salsa Verde (page 119) Mango Sorbet with Summer Fruit Salsa (page 131)

basic recipes

CHICKEN STOCK

Combine 1 kg (2 lb) rinsed chicken wings, 1 chopped carrot, 1 chopped stick celery, 1 halved onion, 6 stalks fresh parsley, 4 sprigs fresh thyme, 1 bay leaf and 6 black peppercorns in a large stockpot, add 3 litres (96 fl oz) water and bring slowly to the boil, skimming scum as it rises to the surface. Reduce heat to a gentle simmer and cook, uncovered, for 2 hours, adding more water if necessary. Strain stock through a sieve lined with a muslin cloth (cheesecloth) and discard solids. Cool, cover and refrigerate until cold, then remove fat from surface.

MAKES ABOUT 2 LITRES (64 FL OZ)

Will keep, covered, in refrigerator for 3 days or can be reduced and frozen for 1 month.

GLUTEN-FREE ✔   DAIRY-FREE ✔   DETOX-FRIENDLY ✔

VEGETABLE STOCK

Combine 2 quartered onions, 2 chopped carrots and 3 chopped tomatoes in a large roasting pan and toss with 1 tablespoon olive oil. Roast at 200°C (400°F) for 30 minutes or until browned. Transfer vegetables to a large stockpot, add 2 chopped sticks celery, 4 sliced mushrooms, 1 bay leaf and 6 black peppercorns. Add 3 litres (96 fl oz) water and bring to the boil, skimming scum as it rises to the surface. Reduce heat and simmer, uncovered, for 2 hours. Strain stock through a sieve lined with a muslin cloth (cheesecloth) and discard solids. Cool, cover and refrigerate until ready to use.

MAKES ABOUT 2 LITRES (64 FL OZ)

Will keep, covered, in the refrigerator for 4 days or can be frozen for 1 month.

GLUTEN-FREE ✔   DAIRY-FREE ✔   DETOX-FRIENDLY ✔

FISH STOCK

Combine fish bones, including the head (preferably from a white fish), 2 finely chopped carrots, 2 finely chopped sticks celery, 1 quartered onion, 3 chopped tomatoes, 6 sprigs each fresh parsley and thyme, 1 bay leaf and 6 black peppercorns in a large stockpot. Add 3 litres (96 fl oz) water and bring slowly to the boil, skimming scum as it rises to the surface. Reduce heat to a gentle simmer and cook, uncovered, for 30 minutes. Strain stock through a sieve lined with a muslin cloth (cheesecloth) and discard solids. When stock has cooled, strain again, leaving any sediment behind. Cool, cover and refrigerate until ready to use.

MAKES ABOUT 2.5 LITRES (80 FL OZ)

Will keep, covered, in refrigerator for 3 days or can be frozen for 1 month.

GLUTEN-FREE ✔   DAIRY-FREE ✔   DETOX-FRIENDLY ✔

SOFT POLENTA

Bring 1.5 litres (48 fl oz) Chicken Stock (page 174) to the boil and whisk in 150 g (5 oz) polenta (yellow cornmeal) and salt to taste. Cook polenta over low heat, stirring regularly with a whisk for about 30 minutes or until soft. The polenta should be soft and flowing. If it is too stiff, add a little boiling water.

SERVES 4 AS AN ACCOMPANIMENT

Best made just before serving.

GLUTEN-FREE ✔   DAIRY-FREE ✔   DETOX-FRIENDLY ✔

BIG RICE SALAD

This salad can be served as an accompaniment to meat, chicken or fish, or as a vegetarian main course, with the addition of boiled eggs or stir-fried chopped tofu.

Cook 300 g (10 oz) basmati rice in simmering salted water for 10 minutes or until al dente. Drain and rinse under cold water.

Cook a mixture of green vegetables, such as green beans, peas, podded broadbeans and asparagus in simmering salted water until tender. Drain and rinse under cold water.

To make a dressing, combine 1 tablespoon chopped fresh chives, 1 tablespoon chopped fresh basil, 4 chopped green (spring) onions (scallions), 1 tablespoon white wine vinegar and $1/4$ cup (2 fl oz) extra virgin olive oil and season to taste.

Stir green vegetables, $1/2$ chopped avocado, 30 g (1 oz) chopped toasted hazelnuts and dressing into rice.

SERVES 4–6 AS AN ACCOMPANIMENT

Will keep, covered, in refrigerator for 3 days.

GLUTEN-FREE ✔   DAIRY-FREE ✔   DETOX-FRIENDLY ✔
LUNCH BOX ✔

ROCKET & PEAR SALAD

To make a dressing, combine 2 tablespoons olive oil and 2 teaspoons white wine vinegar and season to taste. Cook 12 spears trimmed asparagus in simmering salted water until tender. Drain and rinse under cold water.

Place 3 cups trimmed rocket (arugula) in a bowl and top with 1 peeled, cored sliced pear, the asparagus, $1/2$ chopped avocado and 40 g ($1^1/2$ oz) toasted walnut pieces. Drizzle with dressing, toss gently and serve immediately.

SERVES 4 AS AN ACCOMPANIMENT

Best made just before serving.

GLUTEN-FREE ✔   DAIRY-FREE ✔   DETOX-FRIENDLY ✔

ROASTED VEGETABLE & LENTIL SALAD

You can eat this salad on its own for lunch, or serve it as an accompaniment. It's great to take on a picnic. If you are making it a day ahead, you will need to check the seasoning before serving.

Cook 200 g (6½ oz) French-style green lentils in simmering water for about 20 minutes or until tender. Drain.

Combine 1 sliced carrot, 1 sliced red capsicum (pepper), 1 trimmed and sliced baby fennel bulb and 1 red (Spanish) onion, cut into wedges, on an oven tray, toss with a little olive oil and season. Roast at 200°C (400°F), turning occasionally, for about 30 minutes or until vegetables are browned and tender. Combine roasted vegetables and lentils in a large bowl. Stir in grated rind of 2 lemons, 2 tablespoons extra virgin olive oil and 2 teaspoons balsamic vinegar and season to taste. Just before serving, stir in 2 tablespoons torn fresh basil leaves.

SERVES 4 AS AN ACCOMPANIMENT

Will keep, covered, in refrigerator for 2 days.

GLUTEN-FREE ✔   DAIRY-FREE ✔   DETOX-FRIENDLY ✔
LUNCH BOX ✔

ROASTED GARLIC PUREE

Ideal to spread on toast and serve with soup or a salad.

Place 2 heads of garlic on an oven tray and roast at 200°C (400°F) for 30 minutes. Remove from oven and when cool enough to handle, squeeze garlic from cloves into the small bowl of a food processor. Add 2 tablespoons extra virgin olive oil, season to taste and process until smooth.

MAKES ABOUT ⅓ CUP (2½ FL OZ)

Will keep, covered, in refrigerator for 4 days.

GLUTEN-FREE ✔   DAIRY-FREE ✔   DETOX-FRIENDLY ✔
LUNCH BOX ✔

LEAFY GREEN SALAD

We love a leafy salad, made with soft leaves that can go with just about anything. You can vary the flavour of the dressing depending on what you are serving it with, and add other ingredients such as tomatoes, avocado, cucumbers and toasted nuts and seeds.

Combine 150 g (5 oz) mixed soft salad leaves, including butter lettuce, oak leaf, mignonette, watercress sprigs or radicchio, torn into bite-sized pieces. Whisk together 1 tablespoon extra virgin olive oil and 2 teaspoons lemon juice, balsamic vinegar or verjuice and season to taste. Toss leaves with dressing.

SERVES 4 AS AN ACCOMPANIMENT

Best made just before serving.

GLUTEN-FREE ✔   DAIRY-FREE ✔   DETOX-FRIENDLY ✔

BABY SPINACH & POMEGRANATE SEED SALAD

If you are serving this salad with a dish that contains nuts, leave out the flaked almonds. Also, if dairy is not a problem for you, this salad is wonderful with a few chunks of crumbled feta cheese.

Combine 120 g (4 oz) baby spinach leaves, seeds from 1 pomegranate, 30 g (1 oz) pitted baby black olives and ½ chopped avocado in a bowl. Whisk together 2 teaspoons pomegranate molasses and 2 tablespoons extra virgin olive oil and season to taste. Pour over salad and toss gently. Serve topped with 2 tablespoons toasted flaked almonds (optional).

SERVES 4 AS AN ACCOMPANIMENT

Best made just before serving.

GLUTEN-FREE ✔   DAIRY-FREE ✔   DETOX-FRIENDLY ✔

SLOW-ROASTED TOMATOES

Halve 4 Roma (plum) tomatoes lengthwise and place on an oven tray. Brush lightly with olive oil and sprinkle with sea salt and freshly ground black pepper. Roast at 150°C (300°F) for 45 minutes. Serve hot or at room temperature, drizzled with a little extra virgin olive oil and topped with a few fresh basil leaves or other herb of your choice.

SERVES 4 AS AN ACCOMPANIMENT

Will keep, covered, in refrigerator for 3 days.

GLUTEN-FREE ✔   DAIRY-FREE ✔   DETOX-FRIENDLY ✔
LUNCH BOX ✔

HUMMUS

Soak 200 g (6½ oz) dried chickpeas in cold water overnight. Cook drained chickpeas, 2 bay leaves and ½ onion in simmering water for 45 minutes or until chickpeas are very soft. Drain, reserve cooking liquid and discard bay leaves and onion.

Combine chickpeas, 2 chopped garlic cloves, ½ cup (4 fl oz) lemon juice and ¼ cup (2 fl oz) tahini in a food processor and process until smooth, adding just enough reserved cooking liquid to form a smooth paste. Season to taste.

Serve sprinkled with sweet paprika and drizzled with a little extra virgin olive oil.

MAKES ABOUT 625 ML (20 FL OZ)

Will keep, covered, in refrigerator for 5 days.

GLUTEN-FREE ✔   DAIRY-FREE ✔   DETOX-FRIENDLY ✔
LUNCH BOX ✔

HARISSA

Harissa is a fiery Middle Eastern chilli paste, which can be added to many dishes. Whisk it into sauces, add to salad dressings or spread lightly on toasted bread.

Remove stems and seeds from 100 g (3½ oz) large fresh red chillies and soak in cold water for 1 hour. Drain and combine in a food processor with 2 chopped cloves garlic, 1 teaspoon caraway seeds, 1 teaspoon dried coriander (cilantro) leaves, 1 teaspoon dried mint leaves, 1 tablespoon fresh coriander (cilantro) leaves and 1 tablespoon olive oil and process until smooth. Season to taste with salt.

MAKES ABOUT ½ CUP (4 FL OZ)

Will keep, covered, in refrigerator for a week.

GLUTEN-FREE ✔   DAIRY-FREE ✔   DETOX-FRIENDLY ✔

AIOLI

You can add a variety of herbs to this recipe – try fresh basil, dill or coriander (cilantro) or use a mixture of herbs. Add 2 teaspoons chopped fresh herbs with the egg yolk mixture.

Combine 1 egg yolk, 1 clove chopped garlic, 1 tablespoon lemon juice, ½ teaspoon gluten-free Dijon mustard in a bowl, using a small hand-held blender and process until smooth. Add 100 ml (3½ fl oz) olive oil slowly in a thin stream and process until thick. Add 1–2 tablespoons water and process until smooth. Season to taste.

MAKES ABOUT 200 ML (6½ FL OZ)

Will keep, covered, in refrigerator for 3 days.

GLUTEN-FREE ✔   DAIRY-FREE ✔   DETOX-FRIENDLY ✔

STEAMED GINGER RICE

Heat 1 tablespoon olive oil in a saucepan and cook 4 chopped green (spring) onions (scallions), 2 chopped cloves garlic and 1 teaspoon grated fresh ginger over low heat for 1 minute. Add 200 g (6½ oz) basmati rice and stir to coat with onion mixture. Season to taste and stir in 1½ cups (12 fl oz) hot Chicken Stock (page 174) or water. Bring to the boil, cover with a tight-fitting lid and cook over very low heat for 10 minutes. Remove from heat and stand, covered, for 5 minutes. Fluff with a fork, stir in 1 tablespoon chopped fresh coriander (cilantro) and serve immediately.

SERVES 4 AS AN ACCOMPANIMENT.

Best made just before serving.

GLUTEN-FREE ✔   DAIRY-FREE ✔   DETOX-FRIENDLY ✔

PUMPKIN DHAL

This is delicious served with rice.

Heat 1 tbsp vegetable oil in a saucepan and cook 1 small chopped onion over low heat until soft. Add 3 cloves chopped garlic, 1 tsp ground coriander, ½ tsp ground cumin, ¼ tsp chilli powder (or to taste), and stir over low heat until aromatic, adding a little water if spices are sticking to pan. Add 2 chopped tomatoes and 200 g (6½ oz) pumpkin (squash), peeled and chopped, and stir over medium heat for 2 minutes. Add ½ cup (3½ oz) red lentils and 375 ml (12 fl oz) water and bring to the boil. Simmer over medium heat for 30 minutes or until pumpkin is soft and lentils are falling apart. Mash with a fork, season to taste and stir in 1 tbsp lime juice.

MAKES 600ML (19 FL OZ) PUMPKING DAHL

Dahl can be prepared a day ahead.

GLUTEN-FREE ✔   DAIRY-FREE ✔   DETOX-FRIENDLY ✔
LUNCH BOX ✔

CINNAMON CUSTARD

Combine 2 cups (16 fl oz) soy milk and 5 cm (2 in) cinnamon stick in a saucepan. Split a vanilla bean lengthwise and use a small sharp knife to scrape seeds into milk. Add bean to milk and then bring to a simmer over medium heat.

Meanwhile, whisk 5 eggs yolks, ¼ cup (2 oz) caster (superfine) sugar and 1½ tbsp gluten-free cornflour (cornstarch) in a heatproof bowl until smooth. Gradually whisk in hot milk, pouring milk through a strainer. Pour mixture into a clean saucepan and whisk over medium heat until thickened and custard begins to bubble. Pour into a heatproof bowl and cover surface with baking paper. Place in refrigerator until cooled.

MAKES ABOUT 2½ CUPS

Will keep, covered, in refrigerator for 2 days.

GLUTEN-FREE ✔   DAIRY-FREE ✔

glossary

black glutinous rice – this sticky rice is very popular in many Asian countries including Myanmar, Thailand, Malaysia, Singapore and Indonesia. White glutinous rice is more widely used, but the glistening, long, black grains have an earthy appeal all their own – firstly because of their unusual appearance, and secondly because of their ability to combine with sugar and a few simple flavours such as toasted sesame seeds, to be transformed into a sweet snack or delicious dessert.

buckwheat flour – made by grinding whole buckwheat. This flour has a slightly nutty flavour and because it doesn't contain gluten, will result in a slightly denser texture. Available from health food stores.

buckwheat pasta – check the ingredients listing on the packet to ensure the pasta is wheat free. The cooked pasta will have a slightly softer texture than that made with durum wheat and it has a pleasant nuttiness to the flavour. Buckwheat pasta cooks more quickly than regular pasta and will fall apart if overcooked. Check the cooking times on the packet.

Calasparra rice – medium-grain Spanish rice, perfect for paella due to its firm texture and starchy nature. Available from gourmet food stores. Use arborio rice if unavailable.

canola oil – this oil is high in omega 3 fatty acids (omega 3s help reduce inflammation in the body) and has a mild flavour. You can also use light olive oil or macadamia oil if you prefer. All three oils are readily available from good supermarkets.

chickpea flour – also known as besan flour, this flour is made from husked and ground dried chickpeas. It is traditionally used in Indian cookery. We like to use it because it is high in protein and adds a slightly nutty flavour to a dish. Available in health food stores and Asian/Indian food stores.

chickpeas – we like to soak dried chickpeas in water overnight, then cook them to the doneness that we prefer for each dish – in some recipes, we cook them until soft, in others until al dente. You can use drained canned chickpeas instead, but you don't have control over the final texture of the dish.

cornichons – tiny French gherkins, available from good food stores and delicatessens.

cuttlefish – a seafood that has a similar texture and flavour to squid. It is cleaned and prepared in much the same manner as squid. You can find it in seafood stores. Use squid if cuttlefish is unavailable.

five-spice powder – a blend of spices based on the Chinese philosophy of yin and yang, containing star anise, fennel, cloves, cinnamon and Szechwan pepper. Some blends have ginger and cardamom added.

garam masala – a blend of spices, originating in North India and based on varying proportions of cardamom, cinnamon, cloves, coriander, fennel and cumin, which are roasted and ground together.

gluten-free all-purpose flour – we used Orgran brand, which contains maize (corn) starch, tapioca flour, rice flour and vegetable gums. It does not contain soy flour. This flour is much lighter than the pre-mix (see below) and does not tend to give as good a texture.

gluten-free all-purpose flour pre-mix – usually made from rice flour, maize (corn) starch, soy flour and soy fibre, with some additions like cellulose and guar gum. We used Freedom Foods brand, which you can buy from health food stores. Because it is gluten-free, the texture of baked goods will differ from those made with wheat flour – cakes will have a softer texture and breads may be more 'cakey' and a little denser.

gluten-free baking powder – this is the same as regular baking powder, without the addition of wheat starch. Buy this in health food stores and good supermarkets.

gluten-free gluten substitute – contains rice flour along with other gluten-free starches and gums. It helps to give baked goods a better structure and texture. We used Orgran brand, which is available from health food stores and the health food section of large supermarkets. If gluten substitute is unavailable, you can use xanthan gum instead. Check the instructions on the packet, but generally allow $^1/2$ teaspoon for a cake recipe and 1 teaspoon for a bread recipe and sift with the flour.

gluten-free self-raising flour – contains maize (corn) starch, tapioca starch, soy flour, rice flour and baking powder. We used F.G. Roberts brand which is available from Coles stores.

grapeseed oil – a very light oil that heats to high temperatures. It is light in colour and has a very slight 'grapey' flavour and fragrance.

lamb backstraps (eye of loin) – also known as lamb strips, the lamb eye of loin is a very lean and tender cut and perfect for healthy cooking. It is readily available from your butcher.

lamb rump – comes from the chump end of the chops. Ask your butcher to bone it and trim off the fat.

lecithin – is a component of all of our body cells and is present in the myelin sheaths covering our nerves. Lecithin aids in the digestion and assimilation of fats. You can buy lecithin granules in packets from your health food store and supermarket. It is usually derived from soy beans.

lemon-pressed olive oil – produced by crushing lemons with olives, then pressing the resulting pulp to produce an oil that captures the essence of the lemon as well as the olive.

linseeds (flax seeds) – are a good source of fibre and omega 3 fatty acids. They have anti-cancer effects and help correct female hormonal imbalance due to lignans which provide phyto-oestrogens. They can prevent and relieve constipation.

macadamia oil – high in monounsaturated fatty acids (which help lower LDL, or unhealthy, cholesterol), this oil has a light flavour and is suitable for most types of cooking. Available from supermarkets and health food stores.

maple syrup – use pure maple syrup, available from supermarkets, not the maple-flavoured syrup (which is a poor imitation). In addition to giving a lovely flavour, maple syrup contains a small amount of the minerals calcium, magnesium and potassium.

mirin – sweet rice wine, used only in cooking. Available from Asian food stores and some health food stores.

nori – shiny green sheets of dried seaweed. Available from delicatessens and Asian food stores.

panch pora – the Indian equivalent of Chinese five-spice powder, and is a mix of five seed spices, usually brown mustard, nigella, cumin, fenugreek and fennel. It is sometimes called panch puran or panch phoron and is available from spice shops.

pandan leaf – almost every kitchen garden in Sri Lanka, Malaysia, Indonesia and Thailand boasts a pandanus plant, the leaves of which are used in both savoury and sweet dishes. Buy from Asian food stores.

peanuts – if you are allergic to peanuts, substitute cashews or almonds.

pepitas – are green dried pumpkin seed kernels, available from the supermarket and health food stores.

polenta (yellow cornmeal) – made from ground corn (maize), polenta is similar to cornmeal (which is paler and finer in texture). Available from supermarkets and health food stores.

pomegranate molasses – is a thick, dark flavouring agent made by boiling pomegranate seeds until the liquid is well reduced and syrup-like. Used in Middle Eastern cookery, its clean, tart flavour works well with meat, poultry and fish. We've used it as a marinade for chicken and as an ingredient in salad dressings. Available from gourmet and Middle Eastern food stores.

preserved lemon – lemons preserved in salt and lemon juice. Available from good food stores.

protein powder – we used a selection of protein powders in our recipes. Isolated whey protein can often be tolerated by people with milk sensitivities because it does not contain casein and has minimal lactose. Soy-based protein powder is available unflavoured or flavoured. If you prefer, you can use rice based protein powder. All are available from your health food store.

puffed rice – the puffed rice we like is made from a rice flour and water mixture that is extruded and puffed by heat. It results in a lovely crunchy texture. You'll know the difference because the 'grains' are small and pale, unlike the larger brownish coloured puffed whole rice. You can use either. Available from supermarkets (health food section) and health food stores.

quinoa – pronounced 'keen-wah', this small 'grain' (actually the seed from a leafy plant) is cultivated in Peru, Chile and Bolivia and was used by the Incas who revered this nutritious food. Quinoa does not contain gluten and takes 12–15 minutes to cook. Available in grain or flake form, from health food stores.

rice bran – the outer husk of rice grains is high in soluble fibre and absorbs excess cholesterol and toxins in the digestive system, encouraging their elimination. As for all soluble fibre, it helps prevent constipation and also slows the emptying rate from the stomach, giving longer-lasting energy. Available from supermarkets and health food stores.

rice milk – is more watery in texture because it contains very little fat. It is a good substitute for dairy milk. Buy the type that has calcium added. Available from supermarkets and health food stores in long-life cartons. You can use reduced-fat soy milk instead if you prefer.

rice wine vinegar – made from fermented rice, rice wine vinegar (also known as rice vinegar) is used in Asian cookery. Readily available from supermarkets and Asian food stores, there is no decent substitute.

rolled brown rice flakes – are just as they sound – raw brown rice grains that have been rolled flat. They make quite a good porridge. Available from health food stores. You can use rolled white rice instead if you like.

saffron threads – threads from the dried stigmas of the crocus flower. Available from good food stores and some supermarkets.

shaohsing cooking wine – made from a combination of glutinous rice, millet, a special yeast, and local mineral water, shaohsing cooking wine tastes like dry sherry. It is aged for at least 10 years which results in a warm amber colour. Available from Asian food stores.

soy milk – use reduced-fat soy milk and ensure it has calcium added. Available from supermarkets in the fresh milk and long-life milk sections. If you have a gluten sensitivity or allergy, check the ingredients list to be sure it is gluten-free.

soy yoghurt – made from soy beans, this yoghurt has a different flavour to dairy yoghurt. We use it in both sweet and savoury recipes and you can snack on this yoghurt between meals if you like. Available from supermarkets and health food stores.

sumac – ground spice from a slightly astringent, lemon-flavoured berry. Available from Middle Eastern food stores and spice shops.

tahini – made from sesame seeds, tahini is highly nutritious and adds a lovely nutty flavour to dressings and sauces. It is often used in Middle Eastern dishes. Available from supermarkets and health food stores.

tamari sauce, wheat-free – also known as tamari shoyu, this sauce is made from fermented soy beans, unlike regular soy sauce which is made from a mixture of soy beans and wheat. Tamari is lighter in colour and flavour. Available from some supermarkets and health food stores.

tofu – tofu is made by adding a coagulant (like magnesium chloride) to soy milk. The resultant curds are strained for various lengths of time, depending on the desired texture. You can find soft and firm tofu in supermarkets and health food stores. Smoked tofu, a firm textured product, is available from health food stores. If you don't use the whole piece of tofu, place the remainder in an airtight container, cover the tofu with water, and store in the refrigerator. Change the water daily and use the tofu within a few days.

venison – is a very nutritious lean deer meat. It has a slightly stronger flavour than beef but is excellent for providing iron. Do not overcook venison for the best results and flavour. Available from gourmet butchers.

verjuice – the unfermented juice of grapes, with a delicate lemon, vinegar flavour. Available from good food stores. Substitute lemon juice and white wine vinegar if verjuice is not available.

xanthan gum – can be used as an alternative if gluten substitute is unavailable. Like the gluten substitute, it gives baked goods a better texture. Allow about $1/2$ teaspoon for a cake recipe and 1 teaspoon for a bread recipe.

za'atar – a Middle Eastern spice mixture, comprising equal quantities of sesame seeds, thyme and sumac, with a little salt. Available from spice shops and Middle Eastern food stores.

where to find gluten-free products

When looking in your local supermarket for gluten-free products, check the health food, organic and flour sections. Almost all the larger supermarkets carry these products now, but they shelve them in different places. Health food shops will usually have a good range of gluten-free products.

WWW.GLUTENFREESHOP.COM.AU
All the products we've used are available here, with Australia-wide delivery. They will also ship overseas on request.

WWW.THEXTON.COM.AU
Orgran gluten-free gluten substitute is available here, along with a range of gluten-free flours (but not the brand we have used in this book). Delivery is Australia wide, with international delivery available via post.

WWW.GOODNESSDIRECT.CO.UK
A couple of different gluten free flours and Orgran brand gluten substitute are available here. Delivery is within the UK. Note that the gluten-free flour mixes contain a different mix of ingredients to the ones we have used in these recipes.

WWW.SHOPNATURAL.COM
A few different gluten-free flours and xanthan gum (not gluten substitute) are available here. They ship within the US only. Note that the gluten-free flour mixes contain a different mix of ingredients to the ones we have used in these recipes.